"Get this book—read it—study it—pray with it—laugh with it! Our humanity is so visible when we encounter something that is both ritually powerful and awkward. Author Thomas O'Loughlin has done an immense service to Christian communities by writing a readily accessible book on one of those 'dangerous memories' in the Christian tradition—washing each other's feet as we follow the command and example of Jesus."

— Abbot John Klassen, OSB
St. John's Abbey, Collegeville, Minnesota

Washing Feet

Imitating the Example of Jesus in the Liturgy Today

Thomas O'Loughlin

LITURGICAL PRESS

Collegeville, Minnesota

www.litpress.org

Scripture texts in this work are taken from the *New Revised Standard Version Bible: Catholic Edition* © 1989, 1993, Division of Christian Education of the National Council of the Churches of Christ in the United States of America. Used by permission. All rights reserved.

1   2   3   4   5   6   7   8   9

Library of Congress Cataloging-in-Publication Data

O'Loughlin, Thomas.
    Washing feet : imitating the example of Jesus in the liturgy today / Thomas O'Loughlin.
        pages   cm
    Includes bibliographical references and index.
    ISBN 978-0-8146-4861-2 — ISBN 978-0-8146-4886-5 (ebook)
    1. Catholic Church—Liturgy.   2. Foot washing (Rite)
I. Title.

BX1970.O47   2015
265'.9—dc23

                                                2015025002

To Eugene Kennedy, on his eighty-second birthday

—for introducing me to a creative vision of community and liturgy

Gestures sometimes speak louder and more lastingly than words.

—Jean Vanier, *Drawn into the Mystery of Jesus through the Gospel of John*

Contents

Preface

For most Christians, both historically and today, washing each other's feet is simply a curiosity of the liturgy. Probably most have never seen it done, much less done it, and if they even hear it mentioned, it is either with reference to a supposed ban on the washing of the feet of women in the Catholic liturgy on Holy Thursday evening or in a news snippet that Pope Francis has washed the feet of some marginalized group in Rome—a news report whose hook is, what a bizarre thing to do! Footwashing seems peripheral, and surely not worth a book!

By contrast, the claim of footwashing to a place in Christian liturgy, acknowledged formally by only a minority of churches, could not be better founded! It is an action that goes back to the practice of Jesus, and is one of the signs used by John the evangelist in his preaching of the Gospel. In all likelihood, mutual footwashing was one of the highly distinctive practices of the early churches—and expressed the radically different vision that they announced and linked with the coming of the kingdom of God.

And so today when many churches, living in a world where theism and confession are personal options, are seeking out more authentic ritual forms, it seems that the time for a reexamination of footwashing as a part of the liturgy is opportune. Here is an action that allows us to connect with the praxis of Jesus as preached, a witness to the vision of a new social order, and a challenge to embrace discipleship. Living in societies—and church communities—that are riven by distinctions based on wealth, ecclesiastical status, color, ethnicity, gender, and sexual orientation; mutual footwashing challenges these divisions, calling on us to recognize our human commonality and equality as creatures, and the bonds that unite us, in Christ, as sisters and brothers in the Father's family.

This book began life as a lecture to a parish group thinking about their Easter liturgy, and I then thought it would end up as no more than a few pages in some journal of pastoral liturgy. The more I looked at it, the more the topic grew—several academic articles—and the more I realized that this was a topic that somehow touched people, including those almost immune to liturgy. I had a sense that the time had come for footwashing, and that this was something where the big churches had to listen to some of the smaller churches of the Reformation (such as the Mennonites) and some almost forgotten voices from the past (such as the Rule of St. Benedict) and learn afresh its value in the school of discipleship.

Then came, as the result of an article in *Worship*, the invitation from Liturgical Press to write this book. I at once accepted the challenge and have found the whole time of writing a blessing: I have never before received such joyful, generous help and assistance in anything I have written! It has been, albeit usually via email, an experience of the *koinonia* and *agape* of the *oikumene* in miniature; and for this, and each individual, I am most grateful. My first word of thanks must go to the late Kevin Seasoltz, who while editor of *Worship* encouraged me to combine historical theology with pastoral liturgy. Mention of *Worship* leads me to thank Bernadette Gasslein, who as acting-editor made many helpful suggestions that have now ended up in this book. While mentioning Collegeville, I wish to thank Abbot John Klassen, whose encouraging comments were most helpful to me. And while mentioning monks, my thoughts go to two Cistercians: Éoin de Bhaldraithe of Bolton Abbey, Ireland, and Brian Keogh of Kopua Takapau Abbey, New Zealand, who sent me many details regarding the Cistercian interpretation of the practice. Mentioning monastics, I wish to thank Patricia Rumsey and her community of Poor Clares in Arkley, London, for help in the formation of this book. Another Franciscan debt of gratitude is to Eugenio Alliata of the Studium Biblicum Franciscanum in Jerusalem. He not only has allowed me to use photographs of first-century-CE *alabastra* from the collection of which he is curator, but also had photographs specially taken of them for this book. Many scholars have gone out of their way to share with me their research on aspects of footwashing in their traditions. I owe a particular debt to several Mennonite scholars: John Rempel, John Roth, Alan Kreider, and Mike Garde, all of whom sent me material or gave me guidance. I am also thankful to George Leylegian for guidance on footwashing in the Armenian liturgy, and to Vitor Carvalho for insights into its role in Seventh-day Adventist practice. I am also grateful to Catherine Anderson and Sandra Carroll for help on the place of footwashing in L'Arche. Lastly, I am grateful to Colm Hayden, a classmate, whose own earnest work as a pastor in seeking a renewed liturgy has inspired me. As I conclude, I am reminded of the medieval adage: *amicorum communia omnia*. But thanks offered, the opinions and faults in this book are wholly my own.

T.O'L
Nottingham
Pentecost 2015

1

Awkward Moments

Washing someone else's feet is always awkward, indeed distasteful. This seems to be a simple fact of our humanity. We wash ourselves. We do most washing in a private space—and treat it as a private matter. And since many modern Westerners tend to be reserved about any touching apart from shaking hands, the gentle touching of another's feet seems just out of bounds. We can envisage other people engaged in washing all or parts of us, but that either denotes great intimacy or nursing the sick. It is not something we would do in public, with people we hardly know, and it would appear just simply out of place to imagine someone washing even a part of us in the context of going to church.

One can look at this in another way. I often ask my students—to see how sensitive they are to ancient symbol systems—to imagine they are inventing a religion and want some rituals to express its beliefs. They come up with all kinds of things from dances and special meals to going to sports events together, but no one has yet come up with the idea of mutual footwashing. Moreover, I would be most surprised if they did: it just does not fit with our society, our picture of ourselves, or our picture of religion. So, before we go any further, let's acknowledge to ourselves how alien footwashing seems to us, let's own its awkwardness, and let's admit that there is something in us that wants to find a way of avoiding it. Unless we own these awkward feelings we will be unable to appreciate this practice, make sense of this book, or understand Christians who down the ages have sought to defuse footwashing, sanitize it, and almost wish it out of existence.

In the sharpest contrast to this instinct to marginalize footwashing (from now on we will treat this as a distinct noun) is the fact that we, as the disciples of Jesus, make the constant claim that we seek to put his vision into effect in the world, to join him in the praise of the Father, and to carry out his commands—and one of these instructions is that we should wash each other's feet! There are only a handful of commands to the followers —expressed in the plural, implying their relevance to the whole community of disciples—given in the gospel tradition, and washing each other's feet is one of them. We all remember the Great Commandment/Great Commission in Matthew 28:19: "Go therefore and make disciples of all nations, baptizing them in the name of the Father and of the Son and of the Holy Spirit." We constantly repeat, "Do this in remembrance of me" (Luke 22:19) and we quickly link the first command to baptism and the latter to the Eucharist. We might remember "Love one another as I have loved you" as the new commandment (John 13:34), but do we remember this: "If I, your Lord and Teacher, have washed your feet, you also ought to wash one another's feet" (John 13:14)? Or do we note that the references to loving one another in John's proclamation of the Great Supper (13:34; 15:12, 17) were expected by him to be heard in the aftermath of a footwashing? Not only is the whole idea of washing another's feet or someone else washing our feet something we find difficult, but we have a second problem relating to it: it is something that we find difficult even to keep in our memory. The consequences of this are that the aspects of following Jesus that footwashing was intended to bring home to us, as individual disciples and as the church, also slip out of our consciousness.

Hesitations and Fears

Case 1: *A Parish Priest's Worries*

Shortly after his election as Bishop of Rome, on March 28, 2013, Pope Francis went to a young offenders' prison in Rome and washed the feet of some of the inmates, women and men, as part of his celebration of

Holy Week. The event caught the media's imagination and suddenly there was a rush among other bishops to follow suit. However, there was an even more vehement response from some bishops and their liturgy advisers: they shouted that this was not a real liturgical footwashing that the pope had taken part in! Why this sudden concern: why make a distinction between the pope washing the feet of prisoners and a "real" liturgical footwashing? The answer lies in a concern, going back over a couple of decades, of those who were so intent on finding a literal and legal norm in every detail of the Roman Missal/Sacramentary. In that book, in the rubrics for Holy Thursday, they had seen the phrase *viri selecti* (chosen males) and, therefore, had issued instructions that women Christians could not be among those whose feet were washed in the Mass of the Lord's Supper.[1] The pope might do it, so they argued, but it was not at that Mass and that does not change the law! The fact that any ruling that makes distinctions on the grounds of gender is unacceptable in many societies today did not matter: footwashing was to be an all-male affair. And as for the bigger picture that an act of Christian service is liturgy, at Mass or not, did not even enter their heads.

The stories of the pope's activity prompted a group of four friends, all women, to approach the parish priest in a community near where I live to ask that he choose a representative sample of those gathering for the footwashing. He flatly refused, citing the law—a rubric actually—as the basis of his action. This reply only exacerbated the situation. Until the pope's visit to the prison these women had not thought about it: it was just one more ritual that took place on Holy Thursday and, in fact, it was lost to consciousness amidst all the other recollections of that celebration. Now the priest's reaction was seen as an act of definite exclusion and a rejection of their equal standing with men in the community of the baptized.[2] Over the following weeks— Easter now long past—these women, and many others in the community affronted by the exclusion, continued to ask the priest why he took this rule (which seemed, blatantly, to be an accidental hangover of earlier attitudes to who could take part in "ceremonies") so seriously. The priest's first attempt at a reply was a simple one based on a belief that recollection (anamnesis) is really an equivalent of a historical reenactment. His argument ran like this: Jesus did it at the Last Supper to the apostles; they were men; so if he was going to imitate Jesus, then the other actors in the drama had to be men like the apostles. To the priest's amazement, this did not satisfy any of those questioning him: Were there not "disciples" there along with the Twelve (and so, presumably women)? Was it simply an "acting out"? Surely it was more than that! If it was a symbol of the priest's service, did he not serve women also? Is it not an action within the people of God and as such one that should include women? Was not Jesus teaching a lesson to his followers, and is that lesson not applicable to women also? In the end, exasperated, there was a shift in the priest's argument: it would be both "undignified" and "highly inappropriate" for him to handle the feet of women. He could not and would not do it: *causa finita est*. The response was that if women were not included in 2014, they would lead a walkout at that point in the liturgy. Impasse and irony. On the day of celebrating our unity around the Lord's table we have division over an action, intended to model relationships of humble service to one another, being the scene for power standoff.

2014 came and again only men had their feet washed on Holy Thursday evening, and many in the gathering left the liturgy at that point. 2015 came and there was no washing of the feet: afterwards the priest explained that it was "an optional rite" and he was not making use of the option.

One could point out umpteen small mistakes in the above train of reasoning, but the big point is this: we have a fear of the whole idea and, perhaps subconsciously, simply wish it would go away. Also lurking in the background is a sense of "purity" and of the "holy" that is based on the notion that what relates to the divine is the utterly unworldly, and this combined with fears that washing the feet of women in the sanctuary pollutes the temple. We may proclaim our faith that Jesus is the Word made flesh (John 1:14)—God at the heart of the creation—and that we worship in spirit and truth (John 4:23-24)—the world is our temple—but we are often led in practice by darker feelings and barely spoken assumptions.

Case 2: *A Fear of Insurrection*

While for most of the liturgy-rich churches of Western Christianity the action of washing feet has been a rare event—confined to one evening of the year (and a not-well-attended liturgy at that) or restricted to groups such as monastics (nuns and monks)—for many of the churches whose roots lie in the Reformation it is a far more common practice. Here was a "Bible ordinance" of Jesus to be followed, so it was followed often on the basis that it was a way of having "a share in Jesus" (based on a particular way of reading John 13:8) and there is still a debate about this in some churches: is footwashing an "ordinance" or something else? If it is the former, then it is obligatory; if not, then (perhaps with a sigh of relief) it is optional.[3] So in many Baptist churches and among others whose origins lie in the sixteenth-century Anabaptist movement, such as the Mennonites, footwashing at liturgical assemblies was, and is, common. But that does not mean it was without controversy.

A recent study of the practice of footwashing among Baptists in Pennsylvania and Virginia in the eighteenth century has revealed some very interesting attitudes to the human body and to the nature of society and power. Footwashing was understood as an inversion of power in society: the master was seen to become the servant in an echo of John 13:16: "Very truly, I tell you, servants are not greater than their master, nor are messengers greater than the one who sent them." Reading such ideas in the gospel was fine, but a problem arose when it was put into practice and this meant that a white male had to humble himself before a white woman or, even more shockingly, before a free or enslaved African American woman. In a traditional paternalistic society any inversion of the "chain of command" has to be strictly controlled—such as at a carnival, on Christmas Day when officers serve men, or on April Fools' Day—but this was just too much. Washing a woman's feet simply undermined assumptions of social order, which links whoever is in power with the very order of the universe: power structures seem to be, like gravity, there by nature. Washing a slave's feet or, more pointedly, a master washing a slave woman's feet was simply courting disaster: it was inviting social disorder and feeding notions of egalitarianism that were seen as subversive of good order. So footwashing was an "ordinance" but not one that was required of church members, and it slipped away to become a rare and episodic ritual.[4] Religion tends to be a socially conservative force and its normal default is to support the status quo: footwashing was seen as threatening. Faced with a threatening social practice, the community sidelined it, forgot the texts that inspired it, and the ritual disappeared from the groups' memories.

This may seem like an obscure example, but we shall see certain elements of this story, such as prestige, power, hierarchy in society, paternalism, and fear of slaves, crop up again and again in this book. Footwashing not only relates to our bodies, but it also touches on our sense of order and power in society, and as such it is something that we inherently shy away from. But it also testifies to the power of the action as a ritual.

Case 3: *A Fear for Jesus*

What could be more pious, or more unobjectionable, than a painting of Jesus during the Last Supper? After the crucifixion and the crib, it is probably the most frequently portrayed moment in Jesus' life. But the Last Supper is fine if there is a clear link to later eucharistic practices—with at most a basin and jug in the foreground as a nod to the footwashing. But what if the footwashing comes central stage? This happened in a painting, now in the Tate Gallery, London, from the 1850s by Ford Madox Brown (1821–93) entitled *Jesus Washing Peter's Feet*. The painting to us might seem no more than would be found in a pious book, but to its original audience it was shocking. This was neither a misty-eyed Jesus nor an otherworldly iconic figure outside of the gritty realities of life. Jesus is shown working with his hands in the all too human task of washing another man's feet. One can feel the towel and the water, see muscles contracted, and see some cloth beneath his knees to save them. The obviously grumpy figure of Peter is neither saccharine and passive nor has he the pose of a saint knowing he is part of a sacred event, while in the background a young disciple bends down to fix his sandal, and his face twists into the pose one adopts to do this. Such a human Jesus was just too human, and a portrayal of Jesus as a servant just did not fit with his place in the official religion of an empire at the height of its powers and a stratified society where servants had to "know their place." We all tend to re-make our images of Jesus to fit the place in society we aspire to for ourselves—and to the talkative, energetic, socially aspiring middle classes of the time, footwashing and the harsh reality of servant life were not images they wanted for themselves nor for Jesus.

But surely those pious Victorians "knew their Bible" and had read the scene in John's gospel that Ford Madox Brown had portrayed? So why were they surprised? Was it not all there in the gospel when Jesus explicitly embraces the role of servant and asks his followers to do likewise? Of course they knew the text. Probably many could have quoted it word for word as an example of the wonderful humility of Jesus, and they would have heard wonderful sermons on the theme. But the reaction to the painting is an important key to human under-standing. Words can just rattle around in our heads, but the painting, deliberately seeking to appear as an image in the ordinary human world, confronted them in a com-pletely different way. Gospel or not, they were shocked. The painting shocked them, and they would have been even more shocked if they had been confronted with actually watching a footwashing in their local church. The idea that they would *engage* in such an action would have been intolerable. Hearing about Jesus doing something is often peripheral to our consciousness; seeing and engaging are far more demanding of an affirmation and commitment with the whole of our being.

Recalling the reaction to a painting a hundred and fifty years ago helps us to understand the uproar when Archbishop Rowan Williams reintroduced the practice in Canterbury some years ago. Someone remarked that he could not understand why a grown man would want to engage in "that sort of stunt." While I was tempted to reply that it might be that Jesus had ordered just "that sort of stunt," I kept my powder dry! But all these reactions reveal two very important aspects of this activity. First, we see the power of *real* and *well-done* ritual. A ritual that literally touches our humanity, engaging not just our minds but our bodies and senses, engaging us not just as individuals but as members of a group—such ritual really can bring the Gospel into our lives and be transforming. Second, as rituals go, footwashing is surely among the most powerful rituals in the rich treasury of Christian memory.

Before we move on from the reaction to the Ford Madox Brown painting, it is as well to note that recoiling from the reality of footwashing and all that it can mean to us as human beings is not part of some modern shying away from the gospel—we all too easily assume that faith was fuller and easier in earlier times or that the Christians of the first centuries were more intent on accepting the gospel than we are today. Sometime in

401 CE Augustine of Hippo was asked about the way Easter should be celebrated and one of the questions was about whether there should be a washing of feet and, if so, when. Augustine's reply is interesting. There should be a footwashing because the Lord commanded it, and so great a practice of teaching by example should take place at the time of the deepest religious appeal—so clearly Augustine was aware of its power to impinge on us. But then Augustine added that many people are unwilling to accept it as a practice in their communities, while others move it to a less conspicuous time such as the Tuesday of Holy Week or the Sunday after Easter.[5] Footwashing seems always to have been powerful but also threatening, impressive but also a practice we continuously sideline and deprive of its power.

Case 4: *Tokenisation and Displacement*

Recently a performance artist, interested in the silent but self-revelatory conversations that can take place between two bodies, "wanted to explore specifically whether [his] hands could be 'in dialogue' with another's feet" through washing them. So he went to what he described as a "traditional Maundy Thursday footwashing ceremony in a Roman Catholic Church" and his reactions are interesting.

> I felt cheated . . . the priest didn't really wash the feet of twelve people from the congregation. He only concerned himself with one bare foot . . . merely poured a trickle of

water on it and then dabbed it with a "napkin" handed him by an attendant . . .

More useful was the scene I located in St. John's Gospel . . . [John 13:5, 12-15].[6]

The scene that this artist describes is one familiar across the Catholic world since the new ritual of Holy Week appeared in 1956. For most Catholics it is so familiar that its inadequacy is invisible to us: but to Howells it was a joke; and worse, it was inauthentic, a deception. To me as a Christian it is worse again, for it transfers the world of appearances, the little falsehoods that mar our inter-human relationships, into the domain of the divine: into the very place where we should strive for honesty and authenticity more than anywhere else.

But faced with that which is difficult for us, we tend to avoid it. How many Catholic parishes have never introduced this because it was not judged "pastorally suitable" and then the omission became their custom? How many others sanitized it by reducing it to a formality that then vitiated its transformative power? In that artist's shock at being "cheated" is an indictment of so much of our engagement with ritual: minimal performance in a context that sends de facto the very opposite signal to the meaning of our words. How can one claim any truth when the person claiming to act as a servant (for a few moments) has an actual servant to hand him a token towel and another to move an elegant basin?

But the history of this practice is the story of fleeing from its reality and finding displacements to avoid it.

In the ritual found in the so-called Tridentine Missal it became a detached ceremony on Holy Thursday morning (in those days the evening Mass actually took place quite early in the morning to save the priest having to fast all day as he had to receive Communion) but was intended for a "superior" and his "subjects"—so it applied in cathedrals among the canons and in religious houses—and was usually a wholly clerical affair.[7] Most people never even saw it. So the law was fulfilled, but its relationship to the church as the people of God and to discipleship was nil. This is displacement into a safe space where footwashing became, in reality, a prerogative of power and its exercise.

But if power must show, once a year under fixed conditions, a model of humility and service—in effect sending out the signal that *you all* should be humble servants—then should not kings and rulers do it? And indeed they did. So in many European courts, from the emperor in Vienna to the local duke, there was a footwashing of twelve paupers. But it was carefully planned and being one of the paupers became a privilege. More commonly, the actual footwashing was replaced with a gift of money. This still happens in Great Britain today when the monarch distributes the "Maundy money": a small amount of cash (£5.50) plus some specially minted "pennies," which are given to the same number of poor men and women as the sovereign's age, and each receives as many of these special pennies as that number of years.[8] While itself a charming ceremony—and a reminder that the day before Good Friday is the day of the great "maundy" (from *mandatum* [= commandment] in John 13:34) of Jesus: "to love one another"—the whole event is also a witness to our difficulties with what Jesus commanded us to do: "you also ought to wash one another's feet" (John 13:14).

So footwashing has fared rather badly in the tradition: we restrict it to one day a year with a limited and controlled group, we imagine it as a reenactment drama of the Last Supper, we imagine it as an all-male affair or a token display of humility by a ruler who may be preaching that all subjects should be good humble servants, we do it in as minimalist a way as possible, and we often seek to replace it with something far less close to us that does not model new ways of relating to one another. And sometimes we are just downright silly, as when I once saw the Holy Thursday ceremony replaced by a procession through the building by servers: one carrying a jug, another a basin, and a third with a towel. Meanwhile the presider told the assembly that it was to "remind them of the gospel's message."

Challenges and Opportunities

Case 1: *Recovering Memories*

We know that footwashing was practiced in the early churches, but our evidence is meager. The principal piece of evidence is the inclusion of the scene in John's preaching of the Gospel: the story would only make sense within a community, which recognized in the account its own practice. The other piece of information comes from a pseudonymous letter, attributed to Paul, from sometime between 125 and 150. There, in a text concerned with proper organization within a church, we find a checklist of qualities that should be present in a woman before she can be enrolled among the widows —presumably a group who were maintained at the church's expense and thereby were able to avoid a second marriage.

> Let a widow be put on the list if she is not less than sixty years old and has been married only once; she must be well attested for her good works, as one who has brought up children, shown hospitality, washed the saints' feet, helped the afflicted, and devoted herself to doing good in every way. (1 Tim 5:9-10)

In this picture footwashing is part of a culture of hospitality, mutual service, and care of the poor. Our source only mentions widows, so we do not know how widely footwashing was practiced or whether others, apart from widows, were to engage in it. The likelihood is, however, that it was not very widely practiced. Significantly, it is mentioned as a task for women—and so this may indicate that Jesus' practice has already become sanitized within a hierarchical society: they carried out the ritual but in such a way that it reinforced the status quo of power within the larger society and the church. Somewhat later, as we have seen from Augustine, footwashing was ignored by many Christians entirely or else moved to the periphery.

By contrast, footwashing came to have an important place in monasticism. In the document traditionally called the Rule of St. Benedict it appears in two places.[9] In chapter 35 we find the regulations about the brothers taking it in turns, a week at a time, to be the servants of the community. This mutual service in matters linked to the kitchen and the laundry is presented as important, and no one should avoid it except for a good reason, in bringing an increase "in reward and love" among the brothers. The Rule then mentions some of the tasks that must be done each week, and this ritual: "and on the Saturday, when the rota changes, let the brother who is finishing his week on serving duty and him who is beginning his week together wash the feet of the whole community." There was no question that these two monks were at that time the servants of their brothers, as in due course they all would be to one another, but the formal act—built into the weekly cycle of community life—was doing something else. By having a formal ritual of footwashing the whole community was affirming that service to one another was an important part of their lives; service was not just some unpleasant reality that had to be shared out equally. Their community was one of mutual service, and this ritual meant that serving was more important than just "whose turn is it to put out the garbage?" Second, their serving in the community was Christlike, part of their imitation of him in their lives (cf. 1 Cor 11:1). Because they were really serving the community each day of the week, their carrying out this action of Jesus linked their service with him. This footwashing was an act of participation in Christ's action and no mere role play. They were to do their serving, and imagine their serving, in terms of the ideal church. Third, the Rule, by beginning and ending the serving week with this action, was making a point about discipleship: the Christian must belong to a community that is linked together by mutual and practical care for one another.

The other reference to footwashing in the Rule, in chapter 53, is in relation to the welcome to be shown to guests. When travelers arrive, among other things, they are to be given water to wash their hands and the abbot and some of the community are to wash the guests' feet. Washing one's feet—as anyone who has walked a dusty unmade road in sandals will know—is almost a necessity after a journey and, in antiquity, providing an opportunity for footwashing was a key part of hospitality. One can find four examples of this in the book of Genesis: 18:4; 19:2; 24:32; and 43:24. In other situations, a wealthy host provided a slave to wash the guests' feet as a mark of respect: honor is shown to the guest in providing them with this luxury service. It is this custom, this social ritual, that lies behind the monastic ideal: the guest is being welcomed as the Christ—made explicit at the beginning of the chapter by quoting, "I was a stranger and you welcomed me" (Matt 25:35). The monks were to remember the bottom line of this teaching: "Truly I tell you, just as you did it to one of the least of these who are members of my family, you did it to me" (Matt 25:40). After the guests' feet were washed, they were to say, "We have received, O God, your mercy in the midst of your temple!" (Ps 47:10).[10] This implies that the Rule sees this action, washing the visitors' feet, as a sacred activity that brings them into the divine presence. The Rule then adds a telling remark on how there should be a preferential option for the poor:

> Special attention should be shown in welcoming poor men and pilgrims because in them the Anointed One is more truly welcomed—after all the respect that is inspired by rich people is enough in itself to make sure they are honored.

This comment tells us something about footwashing— it shows honor and respect, care and welcome—but also that disciples need to be reminded of the temptation to ignore the poor and the marginalized.

The place accorded to footwashing in early monastic rules, such as the Rule of St. Benedict, shows an awareness of the need to take the example and teaching of Jesus in the gospel to heart and to establish it as part of life. It also shows in the differing meanings attached to it, such as mutual service, mutual love, respect, and welcome, that those early monastic regulators were fully alive to the power of footwashing as human ritual.

However, human beings still found footwashing difficult! So while we have evidence of the continued practice in monasteries,[11] we also get echoes of other monks, such as Columban, being suspicious of any washing or touching of feet.[12] The ritual eventually died out in Benedictine monasteries, but the weekly footwashing survived in Cistercian/Trappist monasteries until well into the twentieth century. It is well to note that in stark contrast to the Tridentine Roman Missal where footwashing was given a single significance, that of a display of humility by a senior cleric assisted by two lesser clerics in the task, the monastic ritual has nothing to do with the humility of power but all to do with mutual loving service as part and parcel of the Christian life.

Case 2: *Learning from Each Other*

We have already mentioned how footwashing was at one time regularly practiced by Baptists in eighteenth-century America, but to see the significance that it can have within a tradition of faith and discipleship we need to look at communities such as the Mennonites. Among the Mennonites footwashing has become, literally, an article of faith:

> We believe that Jesus Christ calls us to serve one another in love as he did. Rather than seeking to lord it over others, we are called to follow the example of our Lord, who chose the role of a servant by washing his disciples' feet. . . .

> Believers who wash each other's feet show that they
> share in the body of Christ. They thus acknowledge their
> frequent need of cleansing, renew their willingness to let
> go of pride and worldly power, and offer their lives in
> humble service and sacrificial love.[13]

Many, but not all—for it would be inimical to their self-understanding to have a uniform and fixed liturgy—Mennonites have regularly practiced footwashing. Very often this has been a part of their community eucharistic meal.[14] Historically it has taken two main forms.[15] One custom is for the congregation to be separated into men and women, and then into pairs who take turns to wash the other's feet. The second custom is for six to eight people to sit in a circle or around a table and each wash the feet of the next person. Understood as an "ordinance," it is interpreted in multiple overlapping ways: as a symbol of Jesus' ministry, as a metaphor for the cleansing of sin—an idea going back to two of the original Anabaptist leaders, Menno Simons (1496–1561) and Dirk Philips (1504–68)— and as a reminder of humility and brotherly equality. In recent years the practice has been declining, but a glance at what Mennonite theologians are saying about footwashing reveals a group who see this as a most valuable part of their witness that they should value and restore to prominence.[16] For example, John D. Roth has written elegantly and convincingly of footwashing as a way of affirming the goodness of the body as a temple of the

Spirit, as a celebration of the incarnation in which the Lord emptied himself, and as helping participants to adopt a posture of service and much-needed nonerotic intimacy between human beings.[17]

There is a regrettable tendency among many Catholics to think that while other churches might have interesting features, in actuality we have little *really* to learn from them or cases where they have got it more right than we have. This is an arrogance that forgets that whenever a division emerges among Christians, both sides lose something! Furthermore, it is also a failure to recognize that the Spirit is inspiring not just all the baptized but all humanity. While we Catholics have formalized footwashing to such an extent that it is almost invisible—how many Catholics would list it as a Christian practice?—other Christians highlight a precious part of our inheritance from Jesus. Groups who practice footwashing as a more normal part of their ritual, such as the Mennonites or the Seventh-day Adventists, can remind us that we can never say "we have discipleship figured out!" but rather that we all must journey on the Way of Life, discovering new aspects and depths of discipleship.[18]

While most of the ancient churches, whether Western such as the Catholics or Eastern such as the Greek or Armenian Orthodox, have seen footwashing as a ritual used in imitation of a moment in the Last Supper, the Mennonites have seen it as an ordinance that becomes a practice of discipleship. Anyone on Holy Thursday

A depiction of the footwashing at the Last Supper from a modern Ethiopian manuscript: footwashing is part of the memory of every church.

with the ancient churches could be forgiven for thinking about it as a pageant acting out the roles of Peter, the other eleven, and Jesus—thereby giving a very visible expression to the gospel story. Anyone seeing a Mennonite footwashing would think of it as fulfilling, here and now in a community, a word of Jesus: "you also ought to wash one another's feet. For I have set you an example, that you also should do as I have done to you" (John 13:14-15).

Case 3: *Learning from the Margins*

Jean Vanier, the Canadian humanitarian and theologian, is best known as the founder of L'Arche with its vision of care, love, and inclusion for the disabled and those on the margins of society. What is lesser known is his rediscovery of the value of footwashing as a powerful way of forming a community within a vision of mutual love and respect. Footwashing is Vanier's "scandal of service": "The fact that Jesus washed his disciples' feet may seem to some people a simple ordinary gesture. To others it is something shocking and challenging. In L'Arche we consider the washing of the feet to be an important and highly significant act." [19] Indeed recently, in 2014, footwashing has been referred to as "a sacrament of L'Arche." What does it mean for them?

Footwashing helps establish the bonds within each community, allowing them to discover their shared and vulnerable common humanity and express their communion of hearts. It is part of their domestic liturgy. It is done infrequently, but when it is done it takes a formal liturgical shape, thereby giving ritual expression to the messiness and difficult realities of community life that they are celebrating every day. Within these communities, where a pyramid model of power could so easily manifest itself—one group active, the other passive; one group giving, the other taking; one the "normal" and the ministers, the other the "disabled" and the laity— this ritual ushers in another vision. It changes the model of society and of the church from that "of a hierarchical pyramid to an inclusive body." They see this "as an essential part of Jesus' message of love." For L'Arche is discovering that "people who are stronger need those who are more fragile in order to help them discover their humanity."[20]

Footwashing also serves another purpose in their communities where the members are drawn from a variety of Christian traditions—and, consequently, eucharistic sharing is often difficult because of Catholic and Orthodox regulations on admitting other Christians to the Lord's table or participating fully in the Lord's table when the Eucharist is presided over by someone whose ability to preside they deny. Traditionally in Christian theology, the Eucharist has been preached as the activity that makes the disciples of Jesus one with him: "Because there is but one loaf, we who are many are one body because we all share in that one loaf" (1 Cor 10:17, my translation).[21] In practice, the Eucharist is what keeps Christians at loggerheads, and in small communities of mixed traditions, it often causes bitter division. For L'Arche this is avoided by having foot-washing as a sign of unity. It is then seen, when all celebrate equally and fully, as a moment of communion through the body in the Body of Christ, an expression of communion of hearts, and a blessing from God. This ecumenical dimension of footwashing, a ritual that can even be a means toward reconciliation between churches, Vanier has taken to the World Council of Churches in 1998:

They were young and old, men and women, metropolitans
and general secretaries, clergy and laity. Some wore western
business suits, others clerical garb, still others the traditional garments of myriad cultures from around the world.
Together they walked in procession to wash-basins on the
floor of the Ecumenical Centre reception hall to engage in
one of the church's most ancient and most uncommon ceremonies: the washing of feet.[22]

One has but to remember all the arguments between
East and West (last 1,000 years) on sharing in the liturgy,
the arguments in the West on what is a valid Eucharist
(last 500 years), and the current bitter arguments in
many churches on the ministry of women, to see that
this was an extraordinary action. Vanier, recalling this
moment when he saw an Orthodox bishop kneel down
and wash the feet of a female American Baptist minister,
wrote, "gestures sometimes speak louder and more lastingly than words."[23]

It is clear that as a human ritual, footwashing has
been discovered by L'Arche as one that brings home to
them their vision of service within mutual love and the
community's people-first focus, but to stop at that point
would not do justice to Vanier's understanding of the
importance of this community activity within a life of
discipleship. Vanier's writings on John's gospel present
discipleship in community within a mystical perspec-
tive. In living together in mutual service, we are not
simply performing a humanitarian work or obeying a
divine law, but such loving service draws us into the

mystery of God's own life. He takes seriously the verse, "Unless I wash you, you have no share with me" (13:8). Footwashing establishes communion through the body with each other; it becomes a participation in Christ, brings our lives, here and now, into the presence of the divine. It is not mere rhetoric when footwashing is described as the sacrament of L'Arche but a rediscovery in the messiness and needs of life of the basic insight underlying all talk of sacraments. Footwashing has a place within the mysteries of Christian life: it can be a door to the sacred and a reawakening of a sacramental understanding of all we do.

Case 4: *Discovering in Necessity*

One of the interesting developments relating to footwashing has been the interest taken in John 13—and what Jesus says about leadership there—by those setting out alternative models of leadership to that of command and control. The name usually given to such leadership/management styles is that of servant leadership. While those who propose such theories never advocate that a manager actually wash the feet of those he or she leads—and they usually miss entirely the notion of everyone washing each other's feet—they are mightily impressed with the image.[24] The story of Jesus' action is held up as an insight into how a successful leader should relate to others in their common organization. While this misses the deeper insights about relationship that should animate a community of the baptized and emanate from them as part of their Good News for the world, it is a valuable insight into the power of footwashing even as a memory. While the reading of John 13 in many churches on Holy Thursday is the cause of tension—how will we do this, should we do it, can we wash women's feet—it is worth recalling that it is being recited at management training days to drive home what is seen as a practical economic message: servant leadership works!

This organizational reading of John 13 has also prompted some Christians to reflect on how their churches and communities are led, and what in particular they can learn from footwashing. A good example of this is the work of Madge Karecki, who reflects on footwashing in the life of Clare of Assisi (1193–1253). The saint frequently washed the feet of the serving sisters—those on the lowest rung in the community—when they returned to the monastery from the outside world, and in this she showed her view of power, service, and care of the poor. Clare's humility was seen as being modeled on Jesus, who was *the* footwasher. Karecki concludes, "If we are serious about our own transformation, we will learn how Christian leadership is fundamentally always an act of foot-washing."[25]

The implications for those of us who know that a well-celebrated liturgy is the school of Christian living are obvious. Footwashing should be a practice that plays a proper role in our liturgical lives. We should do it, and do it well, and then learn from it.

So, Why Bother?

I have become convinced that any activity that elicits very deep emotions must either be very silly or very powerful. Footwashing is one of those things—otherwise it would not have been so shocking when Jesus did it, it would not be something that many serious disciples down the centuries have tried to defuse or marginalize, nor would it be something that even today can be so awkward for us. However, not only the example of Jesus but also the witness of those who have carried on doing it down the centuries point to it being powerful, rather than silly. Any ritual with such power, mandated by Jesus and affirmed as the way of wisdom by figures as disparate as Benedict of Nursia, Menno Simons, and Jean Vanier, should be part of our shared life together finding expression in liturgy. Footwashing is a treasure we cannot afford to neglect!

2

An Action by Jesus?

The default starting point of most inquiries into Christian theology or liturgy is with recollections of the first Christians, the gospels, or the inherited practices of the churches. This is *not* where a study of the significance of footwashing should start. I first began to understand footwashing on a very hot afternoon when I had been walking through the streets of the old city of Jerusalem in sandals. By late afternoon the streets had the detritus of the day—litter from traders and shoppers; rubbish dropped by locals, tourists, and pilgrims; bits of fruit and vegetables that had fallen from stalls and been crushed underfoot into pulp; the odd smelly trickles of water from faulty drains and from open-front shops washing tables and floors at the end of the day; and then

mess left by dogs—that made walking in bare feet in sandals most unpleasant. By the time I could sit down my feet were covered with a film of dust, had been splashed with filth, and I felt thoroughly grubby. As soon as I got back to where I was staying I needed to wash my feet, indeed wash my sandals, before I could do anything.

When was the last time you deliberately washed your feet? Perhaps after walking on a sandy beach or after a summer walk. For most people in the developed world, it is something we hardly think of—it's just part of showering! But we are lucky: there are many places in the world where most people still need to wash their feet after being out and about, and certainly after travel. Just imagine the dust that goes with traveling along an unpaved road, the way the dust gets into one's skin if sandals are the normal footwear, and remember that roads were traveled by as many animals as people and so were covered with dung. No journey, long or short, was finished until one's feet were clean from the road. Thinking about footwashing starts at a very basic level! In the premodern world footwashing was just a social chore, taken for granted by everyone. Footwashing was viewed as simply a regular part of living, in much the same way that we think of regularly brushing our teeth.

With that image of trudging along dusty roads shared with animals and, here and there, crossing water courses with muddy patches in our minds, we can appreciate this detail of a well-known story from Genesis:

> The LORD appeared to Abraham by the oaks of Mamre, as
> he sat at the entrance of his tent in the heat of the day. He
> looked up and saw three men standing near him. When he
> saw them, he ran from the tent entrance to meet them, and
> bowed down to the ground. He said, "My lord, if I find
> favor with you, do not pass by your servant. Let a little
> water be brought, and wash your feet, and rest yourselves
> under the tree." (18:1-4)

We find many other references in the Scriptures to the
need of travelers to wash their feet on arrival, and the
corresponding need to show hospitality to guests, taking the form of giving them the opportunity to wash
their feet.[1]

But washing one's own feet can be difficult, especially if one is tired and perhaps lacking the agility of
youth, and consequently an even greater form of luxury
was to have someone wash your feet for you. Here care
and pampering reached a new level and we find references to this practice from across the ancient Mediter-
ranean world. We find references from Greece and
Rome,[2] we hear of it from Plato as taking place at his
philosophical dinner party,[3] and even a few of the special footbaths they made for the purpose have survived.[4]
Among the well-to-do, one not only got food, drink, and
conversation when arriving for an evening meal, but
also had one's feet washed as a preliminary. But feet are
feet, and so washing them for another person became
servants' work, indeed the work of slaves. Within any
household rich enough to have someone else to wash

one's feet or where offering this service was an expected part of having friends around for dinner, it was among the servants that there was the strictest of hierarchies. There were male servants who ranked above female servants, domestic servants over farmhands, and all such servants ranked above slaves, while among slaves men outranked boys, and males outranked women. It is commonplace to refer to ancient society as stratified, but nowadays we can only think our way into such situations of inequality and exploitation with difficulty. It was one of the most basic facts that God or the gods has not made all humans equal, and at the very bottom of the heap was the female slave. She was the person who washed the feet of those who ruled the household and who made guests welcome with this service. It is worth remembering that slaves were not just poor and downtrodden; they were only accorded the rights and status of robots: think of them as biological robots. And in such a society, where power was viewed as a triangle flowing from a natural pinnacle and everyone jockeyed to hold on to their rung in the chain of higher and lower status, the footwasher is on the floor both literally and in significance.

We see how this culture was reflected in Jewish thinking by looking at the same passage from Genesis as it was translated into Greek, the Septuagint, well over a century before the time of Jesus:

> And God appeared to [Abraham] beside the oak of Mamre as he sat at noon in his tent's opening. And when he lifted

up his eyes he beheld three men standing in front of him,
so he ran from his tent and fell down on the ground before
them out of respect. Then he said "Lord, if I have found
favor in your sight, do not pass your servant by! Let water
be brought and *let your feet be washed*, and then you can
refresh yourselves under the tree."

The translator simply knew that if Abraham was to
appear as welcoming, and genuinely showing honor to
God, then it was not enough to offer water, but one had
to offer the services of someone to wash the visitors' feet.
This linking of hospitality, service, and being willing to
wash another's feet was not simply a Greco-Roman
custom, but also had deep roots within Hebrew culture.
In 1 Samuel there is a story of King David sending his
servants to Abigail at Carmel to take her as his wife, and
she greeted them with these words: "Your servant is a
slave to wash the feet of the servants of my lord"—and
she went off to be his wife (25:40-42). In this story
Abigail is *not* a servant, but by presenting herself as
willing to wash the king's servants' feet she is portrayed
as an ideal, utterly pliant wife. The story only has an
edge if one is expecting footwashing to be done to important people by lowly women servants. Footwashing
was the very token of servanthood, and it was linked
with both hospitality and welcome, and with optimum
social relations among the "significant people" in
society.

A couple of texts from a period just before Jesus' time
show how he and those around him would have viewed

the practice. Part of the fame of Abraham, "our ancestor [father]" (Luke 1:73, for example), was that of his great hospitality and this was expressed in the way he humbled himself before his visitors. We have seen how the Septuagint altered the memory of the visitors at Mamre, but in the retelling of this in the *Testament of Abraham*—a text from roughly the same time as Jesus—Abraham is recalled as having washed the visitors' feet himself! In another version he does so with the help of his son Isaac.[5] In the Jewish theological love story, again from around the time of Jesus, called *Joseph and Aseneth*, the Egyptian beauty Aseneth declared her love for the patriarch by saying that she would become the slave girl who washes his feet—and then she does just that when she welcomes him to a great dinner in her family home. Joseph protests that she should not demean herself but let a young maid do it, but so deep is Aseneth's respect and love of Joseph that she insists on doing this most menial service herself.[6] It is a love story on the surface, but the deeper message is clear: an Egyptian princess will humble herself before a Jewish servant. And, for us, it shows how footwashing was viewed: the most menial of tasks.

In the time of Jesus, being willing to wash guests' feet was an established trope for expressing a model level of humility and respect for one whose feet are washed. This is confirmed by another Septuagint alteration of the text of Genesis. In the Hebrew text, at 43:24, Joseph welcomes his brothers to Egypt and gives them water to wash their feet, but in the Septuagint—which formed the Scriptures of the first Christians—this has been altered to Joseph bringing water and washing their feet himself.

What Did Jesus Do?

While the question "what would Jesus do?" invokes a fundamentalist hermeneutic such that we sidestep our moral choices by imagining a figure within our memory acting in our world rather than seeking out the good in relation to ourselves, the question as to "what he *actually did*" draws us into a valuable historical quest. The strange fact is that while getting to the actual words of Jesus, the much sought after *ipsissima verba*, is almost impossible, we can often get back to some of the original *actions* of Jesus. We do this by observing where what became accepted *actions* among Christians are radically at variance with the surrounding societies, be they Jewish or Gentile. A good example is the way that a single cup was shared at Christian meals. While there were many interpretations placed on this action by early Christians (for example, Paul's view of it in 1 Corinthians 11:25 is very different from that of Matthew in 26:27-28), what was not at issue is that they used just one cup. But this sharing of a cup is wholly unique to the followers of Jesus, and so we can assume that here the practice was in continuity with Jesus. Assuming this practice, we can see that the various interpretations that we find in early documents were attempts to explain this distinctive activity.[7] So, did Jesus wash feet?

Our search for the actions of Jesus involves a circle of interpretation. We start by working backward from the references to those actions preserved in the memories of the churches, memories that in turn were part of their appreciation of their community activities. So it is a search that begins in the memories as they related them in terms of their experience and identity as Jesus' followers. This starting point assumes two facts about groups. First, that group identity is formed by the common activities of the group expressed in the statement, this is what we always do when we gather! And second, while activities, what we do, tend toward continuity, how we interpret those activities is always evolving: we are constantly coming up with new answers to the questions, why do we do this? and what does it mean?[8]

The common cultural background of Jesus' followers included familiarity with people having their feet washed by slaves. For some of the wealthy members of the community (e.g., Chloe's people—1 Cor 1:11) this would have been something that had often been done for them when welcomed to a feast as an honored guest; while for other disciples, whose status was that of a slave (e.g., Onesimus—mentioned in Paul's letter to Philemon), this would have been a familiar practice by either having had to get down and do it for their "betters" or knowing that their fellow slaves saw it as a menial task. Those disciples who were Jews would also have had deeper memories of such saints as Abraham and how his willingness to wash feet was an expression of his awe in the presence of the ultimate "better": the divine. Now we can turn to their memories.

Luke tells a wonderful story (7:36-50) of the reconciliation of a woman who came to Jesus at table and "stood behind him at his feet, weeping, and began to bathe his feet with her tears and to dry them with her hair. Then she continued kissing his feet and anointing them with the ointment" (7:38), which she had brought in a small flask.[9] When the host sees Jesus being willing to let a sinner touch his feet he challenges his identity, but is then reproved by Jesus: "I entered your house; you gave me no water for my feet, but she has bathed my feet with her tears and dried them with her hair." This story appears in other forms in the preaching of the evangelists, such as an anointing of Jesus' head (Mark 14:3-9 and Matt 26:7-13) and of his feet (John 12:2-8) and the emphasis in each case is on the significance of what it says about Jesus and his ministry. It is worth noting that in all the cases it is a woman who performs the action and the action is presented as one of loving devotion. While both Mark and Matthew omit any reference to feet, Luke expands on this detail by contrasting the hospitality of the host with that of the "sinner." So Luke, for one, assumes that his audiences can understand the footwashing as a significant action among disciples.[10]

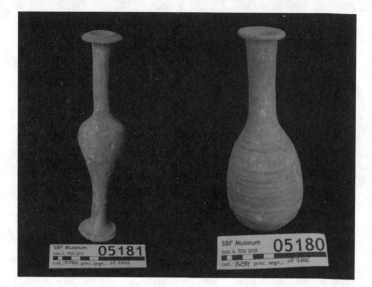

Two first-century *alabastra* found in Jerusalem. So-called alabaster jars
(mentioned in Mark 14:3 [cf. John 12:3]; Matt 26:7, and Luke 7:37)
were actually small pottery containers for perfume or ointment.
Such details remind us of the gospels' setting in everyday domestic
practices.

Then we turn to John and see a story about Jesus
washing feet at the final Passover meal, which is then
interpreted in two somewhat conflicting ways. What
Jesus is presented as saying about the action to Peter
(John 13:6-11) is clearly distinct from the interpretation
given to the whole group (13:12-20). In the first case, the
explanation focuses on footwashing as manifesting a

relationship to Jesus as Savior; in the latter it is exemplary and relates to relationships in the church and disputes about status. All these footwashings take place at meals, all are linked in the preaching in some way with the last days of Jesus' ministry, while in Luke's account of the final meal a dispute breaks out over which of the disciples is the greatest (22:24-27), which provokes this punch line: "rather the greatest among you must become like the youngest, and the leader like one who serves. For who is greater, the one who is at the table or the one who serves? Is it not the one at the table? But I am among you as one who serves"—a piece of teaching, and a location, similar to the second explanation in John.

Later, we hear of the need for a woman to demonstrate that she is "well attested for her good works, as one who has brought up children, shown hospitality, washed the saints' feet, helped the afflicted, and devoted herself to doing good in every way" (1 Tim 5:10) if she is to become a member of a specific group, the widows, within a second-century church. Moreover, from later, usually glancing, references to the practice, it becomes clear that, in the words of Richard Bauckham, "the evidence is sufficient to indicate a widespread practice [of footwashing], highly distinctive to early Christianity, which originated at an early date."[11] Now, what is the significance of this fact?

First, as a group practice it was deeply counter-cultural and must have been held as having some distinctive significance and being somehow a precious custom.

Second, when we read gospel accounts, such as that in John 13, we should not interpret the text in a vacuum—as if the written text is the object of our quest for understanding—but envisage it as a story that was intended to be heard to help its audience make sense of their group activity: the gospel text is subsequent and secondary to the community practice. We need to see John not as a conduit for a curious fact, along with some words, from the life of Jesus; rather he was engaging dynamically with the memory of the community: they were doing this and held it as something that they should be doing as Christians. Now John's story was helping them to locate their practice within their memories of Jesus, their social memory of their identity, and through this storytelling they were investing the practice with new meanings in their present situations. And third, given that the practice was both countercultural and seeking significance—things we can be sure of simply from the fact that John has the story along with two distinct explanations—the practice goes back to Jesus himself.

We can envisage a situation, parallel to other shocking and countercultural activities we see in the Jesus movement, where Jesus did something that, on the one hand, was deeply shocking to those who saw it, and, on the other, was a pointer to the new set of relationships belonging to the kingdom of God. Jesus probably did this many times over the course of his ministry, shocking his audience with the sight of a rabbi, healer, exorcist, and leader of others taking a slave's role (cf. Phil 2:8), and showing them that this was to be paradigmatic

(cf. John 13:15 in Greek: *hupodeigma*) of the coming kingdom (Mark 11:10) where the last is first and the first is
last (Mark 9:35). He wanted to show that in this kingdom
the greatest among his followers must be the servant
(Matt 23:11) and the small fry—"the meek"—would
inherit the earth (Matt 5:5). Such an action would not
only preach more powerfully than words, it would in-
augurate the new age, and it would be a legacy for imitation that would cry out for explanation!

So did Jesus wash feet at the final meal in Jerusalem
or is that John finding a suitably solemn moment for a
sign—for it is clearly that[12]—to act as a foundation-
moment for the later practice? The answer is that such
historical precision is both impossible—the gospels were
not written with a modern historical consciousness—
and distracting: we need to see Jesus' actions not as
one-offs but as symptomatic of his mission. There may
have been a footwashing at that final meal—they would
have had to wash their feet in a busy Jerusalem at Passover time—but there certainly was at least one occasion
when Jesus shocked the group with this action; and in
all likelihood he did it on many occasions and allowed
others who were "impure" to wash his feet as exemplary
of the new set of relationships he was establishing.

Interpretations

Now assuming that the communities had this as one
of their practices when they met and that they had a
memory linking it to Jesus' practice, we can read all the

various gospel accounts as the evangelists helping communities to recognize just how radical was the movement with which they were involved. We can see the
practice as setting a vision of a community where everyone must serve each other, where each must welcome
others even if they are called sinners and where masters
and slaves must see their roles reversed. Footwashing
both binds the community and breaks down barriers.
As such it was undoubtedly a source of tension in the
communities—there were other practices, such as
equality in their communal meals, that caused tensions
in places like Corinth—and these social tensions also
probably explain why footwashing became marginalized and defused into a highly ritualized affair. But the
memory remained and would provoke churches, again
and again, to confront their own comfortable mediocrity
with Jesus' radical vision.

Now we can read stories such as that of the sinner
being allowed by Jesus to wash his feet as a challenge
to those who would not let their own feet be washed
except by someone whom they considered "worthy"
(Luke 7:46). Likewise, we see the humiliation that many
perceived to be part of footwashing to be linked to the
humiliation of Jesus in a scandalous death (cf. Mark 14:8).
The two explanations in John's preaching can be seen
as ways of highlighting the significance of what they
are doing: it is a way of sharing in the life of Jesus (13:8);
it is a modeling of the relationships in the new covenant
community (13:15-16); it is related to the continual need

for conversion (13:10); it is part of the mystery of the risen Christ, which they will only fully understand later (13:7 and 13:16-17); and it is an expression of love for one another (13:34). If anyone objects to this practice, as inevitably many must have, then they can hear the rebuke to Peter (13:8) and they can recall that it is the will of Jesus that they do this to one another. Like it or not, it is what Jesus wants of them (13:15).

Equally, the reality of a continuing practice attracting ever-new explanations may allow us to glimpse a moment in the life of a second-century community in what it says about potential widows. Footwashing was now a task allotted to women, because there is no mention of it as a qualification for the male leadership roles outlined in 1 Timothy, such as bishops (3:1-7), presbyters (5:17-21), or deacons (3:8-13). Possibly the demands of mutual footwashing were just too great for some to cope with, so apportioning it as "the special task" to those who should show their humility was a way out. So just as the lowliest slaves did this in the larger society, so in the Christian society it became "widows' work"—an accommodation that surely appeared consistent with Jesus despite the fact that it subverts the basic communication of the practice. This footwashing survives even when its implicit signals were the polar opposite of its original shocking message. Footwashing was then, as so often it would be later, a litmus test of whether the message of Christ was seen as a religion of comfortable respectability or a witness to the God of surprises.

Ritual, Sacrament, or Ordinance?

At this point it might be good to pause in our reflection on the activity of footwashing and take stock of a few topics that have dominated much of the recent literature on footwashing. It is often the case that one only sees the implication of some aspect of Christian faith by looking at some of the dead ends that have appeared in our formal thinking. The first point is that we can be so concerned with the text of the gospels—deciphering a piece of writing—that we forget that that piece of preaching was secondary both to the audiences' own experience of footwashing as a communal activity and to their more general memories of Jesus as one who turned values upside down. This concern with the gospel as a piece of text in a sacred book, the Bible, means that while there have only been a smattering of studies of footwashing—a couple of books and a handful of articles—there has been a deluge of studies of the text of John: every commentary devotes a chapter to it.[13] But while these may be excellent commentaries on the gospel, they often end up exploring a theme, the position of the story, and its complex significances within the evangelist's theology, rather than focusing on an experience that was common among the audience. If mutual footwashing is a significant experience for Christians, then we should note that the practice and experience is primary, and all interpretations—including that of John—are secondary to that recurrent event in life. Indeed, too few scholars write on John's text as people who have washed the feet of others or who have had their own feet washed. When one meets someone for whom footwashing is a real experience before it is an object of scholarly reflection on a text—for example, Jean Vanier—then the whole approach to what we read in the gospel is transformed and this tale in John ceases to be either a piece of complex theological code or a didactically driven absurdity, and becomes a moment giving voice to a way into the heart of the mystery of our humanity and God's place within that humanity.[14]

If we are to have a renewed experience of footwashing as a significant expression of our identity as disciples and as a harbinger of the kingdom, then we need to start with our experience in community and then read the gospel—and the wonderful commentaries upon it with their layers of insight—as bringing new perspectives to our experience. This would have been the sequence for John's audience, who would have known the practice in everyday life as well as within their Christian community. We too need to hear the gospel in the light of shared activity. Text without experience reduces the Good News to a holy book, while shared experience without further shared reflection reduces liturgical activity to a bundle of cultic curiosities. The same dynamic that John preaches—action and interpretation—should be our liturgical dynamic.

A second supposedly either-or dilemma animating scholarship on this topic is whether or not Jesus was engaged in a *ritual* washing of feet or a *real* washing of feet. Scholars such as Bauckham (whose own study of John 13:1-17 is among the best textual commentaries) is at pains to point out that "those exegetes who see in verses 14-15 the institution of a special religious rite of footwashing miss the ordinariness of footwashing as one of the most frequent of life's chores." He then argues that "to confine mutual footwashing to a ritual context while continuing to treat ordinary footwashing as the task only of slaves would create a scarcely tolerable contradiction in the social significance of this act."[15]

This needs unpacking because, on the one hand, Bauckham is correct, but, because of a lurking assumption of a genuine antithesis between ritual and reality, is apt to miss part of the larger picture. He is wholly correct in that Jesus' aim was to proclaim a new set of relationships: one could not be a member of the kingdom and still be a person who accepted slavery—a religious truth that would only be fully accepted, formally, by many of his followers in the later nineteenth century. Jesus was getting down on a real floor, with real water, basin, and towel, and doing a real and probably much-needed job. It was no mere dribbling of a few drops of water onto spotless feet and a dab with a towel. Likewise, it was showing a new real way of behaving to one another: you could not claim to be one who accepted the last as first and the first as last, and that the leader of all must be the servant of all, and then next day arrive in a household and expect a slave, possibly a Christian sister or brother, to do this task for you: that would be intolerable. Discipleship was to make a real difference in one's life, and had many unpleasant consequences for the social hierarchy if taken seriously. Jesus' action was no mere classroom activity to help him with a piece of abstract preaching. This was a real challenge both to social norms and the accepted assumptions about human dignity—that is, in a society where human brothers and sisters were property and beasts of burden—and implied consequences that were awkward, unpleasant, and expensive for those followers who were more familiar with having their feet washed rather than washing others' feet. One consequence of the reality of Jesus' action is that many of the splendid footwashings engaged in by emperors, princes, and popes down the centuries—a token dribble of water to "model" humility today but back to social hierarchy immediately afterwards—are not simply liturgically inadequate, but are a mockery of the claim to be a follower of Jesus. If one is going to wash another's feet as a disciple of Jesus, then there must be a real commitment to a new set of social relationships.

But reality and ritual are not opposites: ritual recognizes in a specific act, word, or image something that we know is much larger; it captures in a moment a whole story and scenario. We use rituals all the time in our lives to lay hold of life's big realities: ritual is not an add-on, nor playacting, but part of being human.[16] Jesus did *not just* want them to do footwashing; he wanted them to wash the feet of each other *and* to see that this

was characteristic of a whole set of relationships between them as his disciples and a key to a whole vision
of the universe such as we glimpse in words in the
Beatitudes. Footwashing was reality *and* ritual. To use
a (much misunderstood) word: it was sacramental. The
ongoing task for those first Christians to whom John
preached the Good News, as well as for us today, is to
make sure that we keep the connection between what
we express ritually in our liturgies and what happens
in the rest of our lives. There is no disciple who does
not need to learn afresh each day from the parable of
the Pharisee and the Publican (Luke 18:9-14).

Recent years have seen much written on the topic of
whether or not footwashing is a sacrament or a forgotten
sacrament.[17] While the interest in footwashing, and
much of the research into its history, is most welcome,
the debate is rather sterile. It generally assumes a late-
medieval/Reformation era notion of a sacrament as a
fixed rite—almost as a religious object instituted by
Jesus in a deliberate manner. It is a notion of sacrament
that led to endless debates as to whether there are seven
of them, only two of them, and whether they have a
common nature as sacraments. It further supposes a
lawyer's approach to ritual and literalist approach to
texts. Over the last century most churches have come
to recognize that the whole of the universe can be sacramental and all our gatherings and rituals are participations in the primordial sacrament who is the Christ. As
such, mutual footwashing brings us into the presence of

Christ, it can be a moment where our lives are opened to the mystery of God, and by which we are empowered to set out anew in our journey as disciples. But we do not need to put it into the straitjackets of scholastic, Reformation, or neoscholastic debates on sacramental systems. Indeed, one of the advantages of footwashing as a well-attested action within the churches that we can also link directly to the actions of Jesus is that it is free from inherited theological disputes.[18]

So can we call footwashing a sacrament—as, for example, some in L'Arche refer to it as the sacrament of L'Arche? Yes, provided we are not trying to suggest that it should be lined up within the categories of an older sacramental theology. But if we are thinking of it as another expression of "Christ the sacrament"[19] or as a "door to the sacred"[20]—then in this more enriched language of mystery, it can indeed be called a sacrament. That said, the word "sacrament" has such a reified connotation in most modern Western languages that it is probably more fruitful in terms of producing light rather than heat to avoid the term.

Another peripheral debate concerns whether or not footwashing is an ordinance—something that Christians have been *ordered* to do by Jesus and, as such, it must be done! The debate is another legacy of the Reformation period, this time between the Lutherans and Anabaptists. As with the sacrament debate, this is a question that belongs within a dated theological paradigm of viewing the church's memories as a legal code where

jurisprudence rather than religious insight is the exe-
getical key. The question is not whether an action was
ordered or commended or merely a once-off practical
lesson. The challenge of footwashing is to recognize that
Jesus' Good News calls us to a new set of relationships
with one another, and a radically different view of the
place of power in human affairs. Ordinances, commands, non-orders, dereliction of duty, and penalties
belong to a world of religion viewed as a body of legisla-
tion—and that is a part of our history whose limitation
should be a warning to us to pass beyond.

In short, Jesus was a servant leader and at no time
was that more visible to his disciples than when he performed this real service for them. Coming to grips with
it and understanding its implications was the work of
the rest of their lives—and this process continues among
disciples to this day. Footwashing relates to discipleship.
We need to experience the vision of Jesus that we encounter in this action, we must lay hold of its meanings
deep within our being and within our insight, and then
live in ways that follow from it.

3

Mystagogy, Memory, and Meaning

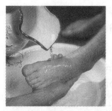 In the last chapter we employed an axiom about human activity that we rarely notice: activities tend toward stability, indeed stagnation, in their repetition, while interpretations and actions' meanings to people tend toward change, constantly embracing new dimensions and aspects. One can see this phenomenon already by the time John was preaching in that he combined at least two distinct interpretations of footwashing. And if we want a more recent, very clear-cut example of the phenomenon, we could examine the altered meanings that Mennonites have attributed to their practice over the centuries.[1] We can see this phenomenon of a repeated

action gathering new layers of meaning, more diffusely, in the number of linkages made between a vestigial practice and baptism, penance, discipleship, humanity, care for the poor, mutual service, welcome, and respect that have been given to footwashing down the centuries. But alongside noting the phenomenon we should pay attention to three other aspects of how humans behave in communities. The first is so well known to us that we have captured it in a proverb: Familiarity breeds contempt. We engage in an activity with great care and attention the first time we do it, soon it becomes familiar, then routine—and at that point we cut corners, forget details, and just repeat it any old way. The practice atrophies, and what was once an important action becomes a quaint marker of distinctiveness whose original purpose is long forgotten. We see this phenomenon all around us, but because worship activity tends to follow deeply ingrained patterns, Christian rituals—even for those groups such as the Mennonites and Quakers who do not set a high value on rituals—abound with vestigial forms. The eminent example of this phenomenon is what happened to the two central and distinctive actions of Jesus' meal practice: sharing a loaf and drinking from a single cup could eventually become a ciborium full of precut individualized wafers while the cup was simply not shared![2]

The second point is that religions live by memory. This remembering is an activity that takes place right now in the midst of my concerns today—so memory is always in a state of flux. Because the object remembered is imagined as a stable fact of the past, we fail to notice that *what we remember* is always changing. We read and reread, remember and remember afresh: and the salient "facts" of our past as we recall them today—and so what they mean to us—are different from what they were and what they will be.[3] This dovetails with the first phenomenon in that as an activity becomes redundant as a practical necessity, it often is still continued because it is ingrained in practice, and now it generates fresh explanations that try to explain its meaning and justify its continuance. These fresh claims for its significance now become its purpose and are perceived as its original purpose. The liturgy abounds with examples of this confusing circle of self-justifying memory. A very clear example is that of adding water to the wine at the Eucharist despite the fact that we have not used that sort of wine for over fifteen hundred years. Now look at the mountain of "deep" explanations found in medieval commentators, the bitter disputes over the practice following the Reformations, or the tortured worries of rubricians lest too much or too little water be added—all working on the assumption that because it did not make practical sense (they had failed to notice that the style of wine changed), it must have a deeply theological rationale!

Arising from the first point comes the need for us to be aware of the danger of letting an important action linked with Jesus and the first followers, such as footwashing, disappear into quaint formality. Which is just what has happened for most churches. From the second point we ought to draw the lesson that we should view all explanations—especially where the explanation originates as an exegesis of a biblical text as distinct from a lesson drawn from an actual activity—as provisional. Such explanations should be regarded as more like rereadings of a poem than a quest for some primordial code or key. Moreover, all rereadings have to be appreciated in terms of our overall understanding of the demands of following Jesus today.[4]

Another lesson we should draw from these points concerns how we grow in understanding through engaging in communal activity. There is a difference between the library or study, whether that be a private desk or a group sharing thoughts while reading the Bible, and the kitchen, the primordial place of doing and acting together. That which emerges from the study is primarily speculative, that from the kitchen is praxeological—and their differences are massively important for our lives.[5] Ritual knowledge involves both kinds of knowing, but we tend both to downplay the role of praxis and to forget that there needs to be a healthy interplay between each kind of knowing. Praxis knowing—such as happens as one washes someone else's feet—is embodied; it involves my body and the body of another, it is active, it transforms the situation we both are in, and it can transform both our social space and my internal perceptions. The action, quite literally, touches both of us. It is a hands-on knowing that should lead to each person having more discipleship skills. Speculative knowing tends to be more detached and cerebral, but while this has been praised in the tradition as contemplative, it has a downside: it tends toward regarding ideas as sufficient in themselves and to be rather shallow in terms of our actual lives. Practice-based learning is, very obviously, prescriptive in that one must do this or that, but it also founds and establishes a world around us. This established world, this culture, is one in which we can live. Language-based knowing is more descriptive of the world, experienced as a fact lying "out there," but it also allows us to dissociate ourselves from that world. Once people engage with the world, the action changes the world and, perhaps in a minute way, brings a new world into being. On the other hand, speculative learning keeps the world at a distance and envisions action as distinct from what we know. We all appreciate this fundamental aspect of humanity when it comes to hiring a plumber to mend a boiler: we expect the plumber to both know what is wrong and have the hands-on skills to fix the problem properly, swiftly, and without too much mess. A plumber who had only read the books would not be what we want, nor just someone who had often used wrenches and pliers. But when it comes to approaching liturgy we very often concentrate on the speculative, see action as a mere spin-off, and miss the significance of the wisdom that is transmitted and received in doing. One can see this confusion of the speculative with the praxeological in some of the surrogates that are thought up (in studies) to avoid the awkwardness of footwashing, such as washing hands, carrying a jug, basin, and towel as props without using them, or, most commonly, having a token washing of a token group done with an air of unreality that we would reject if we were actually in a theater.[6]

Here is a great liturgical opportunity. Footwashing is firmly on the praxis end of discipleship: we can change our lives and our communities by doing it. Doing it together helps us bring about the world that we profess when we say we believe in the kingdom. And it is only when we have the experience of such new ways of acting together that we can reflect on what it means to us, what it tells us about discipleship, and what it tells us about the God we believe in. Footwashing is an instance of mystagogy.

False Paths

Another aspect of praxis-based learning is that we have to take special note of our mistakes, and there are several directly connected with footwashing. The most common mistake—and we have been making it in various ways since the early Middle Ages[7]—has been to imagine that there is a single fixed meaning to footwashing that is then expressed in activity. Another version of this is to imagine that there is a theology that "finds expression" in liturgy—with the implicit corollary that so long as the theology is sound and accepted, the actual expression is somehow secondary. But all genuinely important human skills—relating to living with others, loving, caring, and working for a better world—are learned in shared practice and meaning evolves and gives further expression to the practice. The call of Jesus as heard in John's gospel is that we engage in serving one another, and then learn from this. So the process is to do it, do it well and genuinely, and then ask each other what we have discovered about ourselves, each other, and the kind of world we live in.

The second problem concerns the most common form that footwashing has taken in Western practice since the later Middle Ages, whether that be in the Roman Rite proper or in other footwashing ceremonies performed by kings and princes. In these, and the ritual as described in the rubrics of the current Roman Missal is an example, the underlying idea is that the one in charge does the footwashing as a demonstration that he is really there, deep-down, as a servant (implicitly admitting, once a year, that this is a virtue none too visible normally). Not only does this not respect the nature of who we are called to be as disciples in the church, but it is so full of contradictions that it makes liturgy into defensive propaganda of power structures. Here is how it works as a piece of ritual communication. When a leader—for example, a parish priest—washes the feet of his group (or of a token few of them) and the service is not returned, he claims that this models his relationship of service and humility to those he leads. But this model of humility is based on the passive humility of the slave—who has no choice in the matter. Active humility would be the action of washing an equal's feet or those of a superior! The whole thing is built around a hierarchical vision of society. The Holy Roman Emperor, in days gone by, washing the feet of some poor men, the bishop washing the feet of his priests, or the cleric washing his parishioners' feet all send the signal that "though I am the significant one, and you the lesser, I am also a humble leader." In effect, the footwashing becomes a prop to the power triangle of imagining fundamental inequalities.

But the challenge of footwashing is that *we all experience serving and being served, loving and being loved, and recognizing the new relationships that belong to the kingdom.* We are together creating a community and culture of tenderness toward one another. If someone comes away from watching a footwashing thinking "Father was so humble in doing that," then the liturgy has failed. We do not need a moment's playacting at being servants. What we all need to discover is that in Christ all are welcome, loved, cared for, and that we may find actually living life as disciples far harder than just mouthing "Amen" to a series of questions. In a nutshell: if just one person washes feet, then what is being signaled is a particular kind of relationship within our present society of status and power; when everyone both washes feet and has one's feet washed, we are modeling an alternative vision of society. That new society is the Christian vision of the kingdom. In the first case we are accepting a vision of power but suggesting that it should have a

sprinkling of humility; in the second case we are saying
that the call of Jesus is to all of us to live in a new way.

There has been a wealth of elaborate ritual linked to
footwashing down the centuries—much of it performed
in a highly operatic mode—but it may have completely
missed the point.[8] Instead of footwashing inaugurating
the new world of the kingdom, it was that of a superior
washing the feet of an inferior who, the moment the
ceremony ended, had to be all the more subservient
toward such a splendid ruler![9] The simple fact is that
any footwashing that is done by just one person to several others, without reciprocation, fails to appreciate
that it is about *mutual service*. It is this mutuality of relationships that characterizes the church—and hence
John 13:14 is wholly in the plural: "*ye* also ought to wash
one another's feet." Moreover, the humility of the Christian is not about a servile passivity, but active service of
the other, thereby recognizing that each of us is equally
unique in value and dignity, and no one should experience exclusion or being patronized. Footwashing that
does not have this social edge, recognizing the ethical
dimension of discipleship, is, more likely than not, an
employment of the gospel in support of established
power. Moreover, we are not there even to learn about
Christian egalitarianism as disciples—much as we may
need to experience that—but something even more
difficult: the *other-centeredness* of Christian life.[10]

The third dead-end is to imagine the liturgy as an
elaborate mime, a tableaux recreating an imaginary

picture of the Upper Room.[11] Because this approach is so visually attractive, it is for many the default mode for the footwashing on Holy Thursday night. Then the liturgy ceases to be our own worship and becomes a performance with the presider playing the role of Jesus, some men playing the role of the disciples, and the purpose is imagined as if it were merely a playing out of the text of the gospels. But we gather to celebrate the Good News in the liturgy, not engage in schoolroom drama; we gather to be the people of God today, rejoicing in the Father's love where we are, not to be nostalgic for a moment in Jerusalem long ago. We must learn now from the practice of serving one another and not engage in a lovely, historical mock-up.

Discipleship is learned in the activity of really serving one another. This is brought into fuller consciousness by what takes place in our worship when we, in union with Christ, come into the presence of the Father. There is a place for reconstructions, reenactments, and activities that assist in historical recollection, but that place is in the classroom. In short, dramatization is not worship; but footwashing is worship because in serving one another we are serving God in the presence of Christ.

Part of Our Mystagogy

Mystagogy is one of those words that liturgists use, but which seems far from what happens in the average parish. Likewise, it is a word historical theologians use with reference to the early church but it seems to relate more to what happened in fourth-century Jerusalem than to today. But we encounter many parallels to the process of mystagogy in the course of our lives. After any searing event or crisis that has touched us deeply, while we may try to describe it in words we are aware of both our words' inadequacy and the need to have experienced the event. Some parts of life can only be understood *after* we have experienced them and we have reflected together and give that shared experience words. Even then, any words used are merely attempts to bring out aspects of what we now know was going on: all the later meanings and explanations are somehow latent in the primordial experience and then rise to consciousness through reflection in dribs and drabs. Footwashing belongs to mystagogy, because it is only after we have experienced it that we can talk about it, yet all the subsequent talking cannot replace the action! The event is the act of doing it; and if we have done it we will realize that we have changed through doing it and have learned through doing it.

So what is mystagogy? It is a process by which we, as a community, learn the ways of God through rich human events and then through reflecting on those events we find words for what we have done together and how those actions link us with Christ. Footwashing has its specific value for Christians because Jesus engaged in it and wanted us to learn through engaging in it. As an action it is latent with possibilities and to some of these possibilities we can give words. Through our familiarity with the practice we can appreciate the gospel's call afresh and through the activity have a share in the life of Christ. Footwashing, like all interpersonal actions that touch us, is for Christians a symbol; and, as such, it can give rise to endless new reflections as we try to fathom the mystery of God's involvement with us in Jesus.

The Lord Is Present

That last point is worth stressing: Christ is present among us when we wash each other's feet. This is not the visual magnificence of a celebration of Christ's presence such as we see in an altar decked out for exposition in a monstrance or the celebration of Christ's presence by analogy with the arrival of a medieval prince that gives us the form of traditional Corpus Christi processions. Nor is it the individualist and contemplative presence of a tabernacle in a dimly lit church. These have been the dominant themes in most Catholic expressions of Real Presence in recent centuries. Likewise, it is not the presence of the Lord that is celebrated in the Liturgy of the Word and in words and books—the dominant expression of the notion of presence in most Reformed churches. Footwashing celebrates Christ's presence in ourselves and other people in our sharing and community, in our interaction and acts of love toward one another. It is the presence of the Logos who has become an individual human being in the messiness and the awkwardness of life, experiencing stiff joints, wrinkled feet, and, oftentimes, embarrassment.

This is the Christ "among [us] as one who serves" (Luke 22:27). He is present in the one who is washing feet and in the one whose feet are being washed. In the mutuality of other-centeredness we may encounter him in a new way. If "lay[ing] down one's life for one's friends" (John 15:13) is the ultimate in other-centeredness, and we see in that act both a key to the death of Jesus and our vocation—"We know love by this, that he laid down his life for us—and we ought to lay down our lives for one another" (1 John 3:16), then the act of washing another's feet can be seen as setting out on a pathway of discipleship. Moreover, in celebrating the presence of the Lord on a damp floor among wrinkled feet that have trod many difficult roads in their lives, we come to a new, and in its own way, radiant vision of who Jesus is.

Footwashing and the Basis of *Christian* Liturgy

All ancient religions set great store on the notion of borders: who can enter the temple, who must remain outside, who can come inside, and who is only partially so. We see all this in the complex regulations that governed access to the temple: there was the court of the Gentiles, then women, then men, then priests, and, finally, the Holy of Holies reserved to the High Priest alone. Borders and boundaries were the visible expression of worship. Cult expressed its holiness in its exclusivity and by being divisive. But our vision of liturgy is radically different: the curtain of the temple has been torn apart (Mark 15:38) and the time has come when one hill is the same as another, "when the true worshipers will worship the Father in spirit and truth" (John 4:20-24). Our liturgy must be about breaking down the borders that set up divisions with those around us, in the church and in the larger society, and through actions like footwashing—which breaks the expectations and borders within human groups—we affirm that distinctively Christian vision.

In an early medieval baptismal ritual from Spain, there is an instruction to the bishop that he should wash the feet of the newly baptized and then interpret his action to them with these words: "I am washing your feet, just as our Lord Jesus, the Christ, washed the feet of his disciples; now you too must do likewise and wash the feet of strangers and travellers in order that you might obtain eternal life."[12] Here we have a snapshot of the Christian way: faith and baptism must issue out in the demands of the way of discipleship; we have been made welcome, and we pass this on to whomever we meet; and footwashing grounds us in this process. When we engage in this activity one to another, we are affirming a specifically Christian way of being together, of our mutual dignity as the baptized, of who we are as the community of the church, of our vision of what will bring about the kingdom; and we are declaring that we are committed to being on the side of the poor, the suffering, the excluded, and those in need of an experience of God's loving mercy.

4

Getting Down to It

Deeds and Words

The Western theological tradition is at its best when it is in analytical mode, first in the study, then in the lecture hall, and finally in the pulpit. It tends to favor words and concepts over deeds: actions can seem to be little more than ideas working themselves out in visible ways. This has meant that we tend to devalue rituals over intellectual convictions, whether such mental states are called faith or assent. In some churches this has meant a virtual by-passing of ritual in favor of words, where formal liturgy is formally suspect. In other churches it has led to a minimalist approach to ritual where tokens take the place of real objects and deeds, and where verbal formulae are sacrosanct. Western (or Roman Rite) Catholicism is a good example of this where no one worries about precut tiny individual wafers instead of a proper loaf for the Eucharist or omitting the cup from all but the presider, but there is mighty concern over every syllable of the words of institution and how to translate them. But in virtually every church it means that ritual actions are viewed as mimes, mere visual stimuli, or role-plays, communications intended for children or the simple, while there is a constant concern over "meaning." How often have two Christians come to blows over conflicting meanings while both have failed to appreciate the inadequacy of their practice? But we humans are bodily creations, and it is in our bodies that we experience, discover, and learn. We are also ritual animals and we are formed through our ritual repetitions, so the more adequately we celebrate with our senses, the totality of our bodies, the more we experience new worlds. We know this in our everyday lives, we are bombarded with this truth of our humanity every time we enter a visitor experience, a restaurant, or a fun park, but we tend to forget it when we do liturgy.

If a human interactive experience is genuine, then meanings follow, for we abstract them from the experience through our shared humanity. If we start with a "meaning" and then seek to embed it to facilitate communication, we end up playing games that appear silly and then arguing about which meaning—for meaning is always manifold—is paramount. Moreover, the liturgy takes on an artificial tone that is inappropriate to a Catholic understanding of ritual: human authenticity should be the hallmark of all that takes place in the presence of Christ (Matt 18:20) before God (Heb 9:24).

The sequence should be:

Do

Do adequately

The group and each individual experiences and learns through doing

We reflect on the significance of what we have done together

This is the same sequence we find in John 13: Jesus is portrayed as first washing the disciples' feet (vv. 4-5), then he asked if they understood the action that had been done to them (v. 12), and then he offered his teaching (vv. 13-16).

An Ideal Situation

Footwashing, as we have noted, is both unfamiliar to most Catholics and awkward for everyone. But the basic instruction about the activity is clear: all present should wash the other disciples' feet, and all should have their feet washed by other disciples. This requires space, practical materials such as jugs and basins, a certain familiarity with the practice so that some people can take the lead in the activity, and an "escape hatch" so that anyone who simply finds carrying out John 13:14 beyond what he or she can cope with can withdraw at this point without feeling rejected. Dealing with those who cannot stand the idea is a real problem demanding sensitivity, but we have to be careful that a group who say "this is not for me" do not exercise a veto on the ritual. This has happened far too often in the history of the liturgy—we probably already have an echo of it in the text of John when Peter is unwilling to take part in Jesus' action—and it ends up in minimalist, overly wordy, and conceptualist events that neither proclaim the Gospel nor touch people in the depths of their humanity. So it is best if the person who leads the liturgy acknowledges that this is awkward, but presents it as part of the challenge of discipleship, just as a renunciation of individual power is part of the cost of discipleship. Furthermore, while the leader should acknowledge that some just cannot take part—perhaps for medical reasons—this should be seen as a temporary and extraordinary state and that for today they might like to fetch pitchers of water and tidy up after their sisters and brothers.

The shape of the liturgical space can often be the greatest barrier to an authentic footwashing. In older buildings often there is only limited open space, perhaps around the eucharistic table or in the aisles. So it is worth considering whether this is a liturgy that is best suited to an adjacent hall. Wherever it takes place, being able to be in groups of eight to twelve works best. In a group of less than eight there is too high a possibility that the footwashing is just within a single family or between close friends (as distinct from being brothers and sisters in Christ), and, practically, too many groups require too many basins, jugs, and spaces where the washing can take place. If it is more than twelve, then the round of washing and being washed takes too long and taxes people who often have a clock ticking in their heads about how long a liturgy should last.

The simple way, space allowing, is for people to sit in a circle, and have people already deputed to act as the focus for each circle. When the circle is formed, two then go to where there are pitchers of water, basins, and toweling. The deputed person then washes the feet of the person sitting to her or his right.[1] That second person, whose feet have been washed and dried, then washes the feet of the next person. This continues until the feet of the last person in the group are washed; this person then washes the feet of the first person.

What Do You Need?

1. *Basins*

As many basins as there are groups are needed. The ideal basin is the plastic washing-up basin that is used in a sink when crockery is being washed by hand. There are several reasons for opting for such an object. First, their cylindrical profile makes them easy to move and hard to topple. Hence they are far more stable when being moved about on a floor, usually by dragging. The more traditional hemispherical bowl-shaped hand basin is not good on a floor; they were designed for use on a stand; and they all too easily tip over, spilling water if a foot accidentally hits the rim or if they snag while being moved.

People can be asked to bring one from home, but this demands extra planning and there is always the danger that people will want to vie with one another and present "the best." The very ordinariness of a washing-up basin brings our liturgy into the world of the everyday, and the everyday into the sacred domain. It is a physical expression that in Christian liturgy the curtain of the temple has been sundered (cf. Mark 15:38) and all life offered the potential of being brought within the economy of salvation.

By contrast, many church suppliers sell elegant earthenware basins and jugs especially for footwashing. These are to be avoided for four reasons. First, earthen-

Plastic basins are ideal for dragging on the floor with the least risk of spillages. They are cheap, stackable for storage, able to withstand rough handling, and virtually unbreakable.

ware or, worse, glass can be broken and, with people in bare feet, this is problematic and dangerous (and expensive!). Second, they are hard to move about on a floor where the easiest way to move the basin from person to person is to drag it without lifting it off the floor. Third, they are expensive and so foster the notion that footwashing is best left to a representative few. And, fourth, they foster an aesthetic whereby the objects of the liturgy have minimal resonance with ordinary life.

2. *Jugs*

One needs at least as many jugs as basins, but ideally about three jugs to every two basins. The reason for the extra jugs is that any jug that can hold enough water to pour over sixteen feet (if people are in groups of eight) will be so heavy or full as to be unwieldy and likely to spill. It is far better to have extra slightly smaller jugs, which are not so full and can be refilled during the footwashing. A member of the group whose feet are washed or is more than one away in line can perform the additional service of fetching extra water.[2] In practice, *any jug containing more than two liters/seventy fluid ounces will be too heavy* to place on the floor and manipulate without difficulties of one sort or another. Experience will show the most convenient number and size of jugs, but one has to be careful of the tendency to reduce everything to token amounts, a mere dribble, which removes the act from reality and turns it into a "cheat."[3] It is no use restoring a ritual while simultaneously making it but a token gesture.

The ideal shape is that which is used for water pitchers on school tables. As with the basins, plastic is the ideal material. Again, glass and earthenware are to be avoided, for the reasons already mentioned, and because the additional weight makes them harder to use. Again, the jugs used should be the normal sort of pitcher one would see on a table, not one made to some special design that just serves to separate liturgy and life.

3. *Water*

Cold tap water will probably be too cold for many people: the experience is to be one of washing and being washed, not of a shock from cold water! Someone needs to make sure that the supply of water is comfortable, which means the water is around 90°F (between 30° and 35°C).

Very often it is suggested that something be added to the water—I have seen flower petals and scents added—but this distracts from the central message, makes it more complex to organize, and has the effect of taking a very basic activity away from the ordinariness of our humanity.

4. *Towels*

Because John portrays Jesus as removing his outer garment and girding himself with a towel, these actions have been mimed in many highly stylized footwashings, but it is about a mutual human experience and not about mime. Since towels will be needed aplenty, and since many people will not wish to use the towel used by another, and then there is the expense of laundry and the bother of storage, the simplest answer is to use paper kitchen towels: one roll per group. Each, then, can have a fresh piece of toweling, it will dry the feet more efficiently than by rubbing, and it can be used to mop up spills as they occur.

The paper towels can easily be disposed of as paper for recycling or added to compost!

5. *Bins*

At least two bins are needed, preferably made of plastic.

One of these is to gather up the paper towels—and someone needs to take this on as his or her service to the community—and an ordinary wastepaper basket will serve the purpose. Ideally, there should be one wastepaper basket per group.

The other needs to be larger—the sort used to hold garbage—and preferably should have handles on each side. This is needed to carry away the water from the basins. This is needed for two reasons. First, some of the basins will need to be emptied while the washing is in progress lest they become over full and hard to manage. Second, when the footwashing is over, if the several basins are carried to a sink, one is asking for trouble with spillages or for someone to let a heavy basin, full

This forty-liter trug has seen service in both the garden and the liturgy.

of water, slip! The solution is for two able-bodied people to go from group to group and empty the basins into the large bin, which is then carried away for disposal. The ideal is a forty-liter (or ten-gallon) plastic trug (tub)—the sort used by builders for rubble—because anything larger is hard to manage.

6. *Floor Cloths/Sponges*

Washing feet is a messy business! There will be spills, splashes, and wet footprints. So there needs to be some mopping-up kit readily at hand, and someone deputed to bring it to the groups when they are tidying up at the end of the washing. Carrying bins, trugs, and mopping-up materials can be assigned to those who cannot join in the actual washing on a particular day. Again, paper towels can be more convenient than more elaborate tools such as one would use if washing a floor.

How Does One Wash Feet?

This is an inevitable question, and one that cannot be answered by an appeal to some abstract ideal. Virtue lies in a middle course between the sort of thorough scrubbing of the feet one might perform after walking for a day in sandals, on one extreme, and the sort of miming often seen in the liturgy—a few drops of water let fall on a foot that are then dabbed away—at the other extreme. If one holds the foot with one hand over the basin, pours over it some water, and then rubs it around the foot with both hands, that will do. This is then repeated for the other foot. It is far more practical to wash another's feet by pouring water over them when held over the basin than by asking the person to lower his or her foot into a basin in which there is already water. The basin is merely a receptacle for the water that has been used.

One Foot or Both Feet?

In the formal regulations set out in the Tridentine Missal for this service—which assumed it was being done in a location of many clergy: a team doing the token washing and virtually always clerical feet being washed—it was deemed sufficient to wash merely the right foot! But the obvious meaning of the story in the gospel is that Jesus washed both feet—if slaves had done anything less when guests arrived at a household, they would have been in trouble! When I wash my feet, when an ancient slave washed a visitor's feet, when Jesus had his feet washed or washed the disciples' feet—it is assumed that *both* are washed. So act accordingly!

The moment someone suggests that it is enough to wash one foot, then you have heard the voice of tokenism: the least possible action that will tick the box. If ticking a box is what you want to do, then that is fine; but if you want to have a ritual that speaks and challenges transformation, you will avoid that siren comment.

Kissing the Feet?

Some still suggest—often as a rationale for avoiding the practice—that the washed foot, note the singular, has to be kissed by the celebrant. Again this is a hangover from the Tridentine ritual where the emphasis was on miming, within an elaborate choreography, a scene from the gospel. In this case, the scene in John was conflated with the actions of the woman in Luke 7:38 who washed Jesus' feet with her tears, wiped them with her hair, kissed them, and anointed them with ointment.[4]

The aim of footwashing as a liturgical action is to carry out an act of service to one another such as we hear about in John 13—so the emphasis is on an activity of mutual service. That woman's action is best regarded as a unique historical event, rather than as a paradigmatic action. The account in Luke's gospel does, indeed, point obliquely to the significance that early communities attributed to footwashing, but does not mean we should mimic it.

Announcements

One of the inherent qualities of a ritual is that it is familiar; it is "what's done." This may be a genuinely ancient tradition or it may be just what people are expecting: "tradition" can often be little more than something that happened once and something you would like to happen again! Therefore, while some people like surprises, for most people who engage in worship, surprises are disruptive. And people experiencing a sense of disruption—and a footwashing is going to be discomfiting—are not going to be in a positive frame of mind to discover new dimensions of discipleship. This has to be balanced by the fact that one of the aspects of footwashing is that it does mark the social disruption that is the encounter of our inherited views of community and those we proclaim as belonging to the kingdom. So a community about to introduce a mutual footwashing must walk a "kerygmatic tightrope" that is as old as the ministry of Jesus.

A community can take two practical steps toward addressing this problem. The first is to introduce the ritual gradually to small groups at events involving a high level of personal buy-in. A group that performs a special ministry in the community, for instance that of reader, when gathered for a session where they reflect on their ministry and its place in the larger scheme of the church's mission, is far more likely to be positively receptive to apparently new practices than a whole congregation on Holy Thursday. These small groups then act as a leaven in the wider community, showing others that they can engage in this without fear.

The second key is to make everyone aware that a footwashing is going to take place as a part of a liturgy. While one could argue that in John's gospel the action of Jesus is presented as a surprise, one might add that everyone present was far more familiar with footwashing—by someone such as a maid or a slave—than we are: their surprise was not the footwashing per se but that the Master did it, and, moreover, John's audience would have been familiar with their own practice as a group of disciples as they listened to John's story. The fact is that if a footwashing is going to take place, people, especially women, need to wear clothing that is suitable, and most people will want to have a sense that their feet are already washed! This might make the whole idea seem silly to some: if everyone is going to wash their feet and make sure that there are no embarrassing smells or dirt, then it is all just a sham. This objection is only valid on the assumption that all human ritual is a sham: for example, if we are friends we do not need to shake hands when we greet, and if we are not friends it is falsehood to pretend we are by doing so. If we have all eaten at home as individuals or families, then why have a ritual communal meal at which to thank the Father in Christ? However, we engage in ritual not out of day-to-day practical necessity, but out of the greater need to form with others that world of imagination, faith, and hope that we, as Christians, believe is the anticipation of the kingdom of God. As the 1972 document *Music in Catholic Worship* states, "Good celebrations foster and nourish faith. Poor celebrations weaken and destroy it."[5]

But there is a less observed problem with giving too much notice of any liturgical action: the announcement can take the form of a catechesis, which implies that the action has just one meaning or is a practical demonstration of the abstract theological point being outlined in the notice. We need to alert people to the fact of a group activity before the event, but we should not prime them as to what it means: part of the value of a powerful ritual is what we elicit about the mystery of faith through actually doing it. So the notice given should take the form of announcing the fact: as disciples we will wash one another's feet on . . . Then simply offer some verses from the gospel to act as both background and justification. The text should be the minimum: John 13:1-5 and 12-15 with the two passages separated by a . . . It can sometimes be a good idea to use a translation that is different from that heard in the liturgy, as it presents familiar phrases with freshness. Here is my translation:

> While they were at supper, Jesus stood up. He took off his coat and wrapped himself in a towel. Then, when he had put water into a basin, he set to wash the feet of each of his disciples, drying them with the towel tied around his waist. When he had finished washing their feet, he went back to his place at the table and spoke to them. He asked them a question: "Have you any idea what I have been doing just now? You address me as 'master' and as 'lord'—and rightly so because I am your teacher and lord—but do you see that if I, your lord and teacher, have gotten down on the floor and washed your feet, then you should be ready to wash each other's feet? You have seen what I have done, that should be an example to you all: you all should be ready to do to one another what I have done to each of you."

But . . . All the Mess!

Different types of pastoral activity evoke different responses and different responders. If a liturgy is too long, one will hear about it in a different way from the hornet's nest a homily may stir up among those who see themselves as the vigilantes of orthodoxy. A change in the car parking arrangements is liable to cause a riot while there is widespread reluctance to engage with new hymns. However, there are certain actions, such as introducing a real fire for the Easter Vigil or anything involving the movement of furniture, where the loudest cries of protest will come from those who know that the liturgy was perfect some time ago, and that it has been downhill for the last decade or so. Yesteryear, along with youth, is usually golden in memory. And the custodians of such memories are often those upon whom a community relies for the background work of the liturgy: the sacristan and those who help the sacristan. Hence goes up the cry that this is far too much mess, too much fuss, and an insight relating to pastoral theology is usually thrown in such as that it is of little value anyway.

There is an answer to such cries: it is not for those who are happy and content that we seek a more authentic liturgy, but those who are voiceless in liturgy, those to whom the liturgy says little and who, as a consequence, passed away from liturgy without murmur. Yes: footwashing is very messy. Life is full of mess—awaiting redemption. But in the very messy and awkward situation of washing each other's feet, we can discover new aspects of discipleship and find a new way of having a share within the mystery of Christ (John 13:8).

5

Liturgical Scenarios

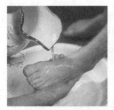 If you have read thus far in this book, you may have come to the opinion that it is a great pity that footwashing was marginalized, in one way or another, down the centuries. But this peripherality has a positive side: this is a community practice upon which the canonists have not built up a massive dossier on what can and can't be done, what it must mean and cannot mean, nor have they been able to freeze one culture or period's interpretation as somehow universal. Very often we have to painfully unpick centuries of scar tissue before we have the precious kernel that needs to be brought again into the light! Footwashing is—Holy Thursday aside—a *Christ*-ian ritual, for within our tradition we can locate it in the deeds and words of Jesus, that is also brimming

over with possibilities for us in our celebrations of our pilgrimages of faith. We have seen, in chapter 1, how one group of Christians, L'Arche, has taken this freedom and used it within their own domestic settings and also how Jean Vanier has used it as part of the kerygma in such settings as a meeting of the World Council of Churches and as a way of incarnating a mystical approach to Christian faith founded in his reading of the Gospel of John. But footwashing is a challenge to every community of believers, a call from Jesus to be taken up and given life in celebrations.

For most Christians, footwashing is a form whose value and significance is awaiting discovery. What follows are just some ideas to stimulate discussion in community groups and liturgy committees.

Holy Thursday Evening

This is the one occasion each year on which there is a footwashing of some sort in many places. It is usually done in mime mode—as if one is acting out a historical detail of the Last Supper—though this is far less obvious in the 1969 Roman Missal than in those that preceded it. So the first thing to note is that one is not bound (if one wants to be very legalistic in one's approach to rubrics) by accidentally inherited practices such as "twelve and only twelve," "only the right foot," or "the foot has to be kissed": these are simply not mentioned.

That said, taking the word *viri* as if it were an alternative to *homines* and so excluding women fails both as a pastoral reality and theologically: this is a practice among disciples—so all the baptized—not among "look-alikes" who can play the role of the Twelve as if we are still viewing the ceremony in the medieval manner of a small-scale mystery play. Equally, taking the reference to the presider and his chasuble as the only way to perform this action fails for the same reason: we are to do what the gospel instructs—wash one another's feet taking Jesus as our example—not imagine that the presider is acting out the part of Jesus. So the ideal development in practice from the 1969 Missal is that at this point all should wash each other's feet in groups of eight to twelve.

And, of course, it should go without saying that anyone familiar with canonical jurisprudence knows that in most cases, unless it is explicitly stated that women, *qua tale*, are excluded, *viri* is to be taken as merely a verbal variation on *homines*![1]

One final point there is very often a crypto-canonist lurking in the sacristy who says that the book must be interpreted rigorously. Rather than seek to train that person in a more flexible jurisprudence along with instilling a more dynamic vision of pastoral liturgy, it is sufficient to notice that since this entire rite is only to be carried out if the pastoral circumstances permit it (*ubi ratio pastoralis id suadeat*), it can be omitted. Since it can be omitted, it is not necessary. Since it is not necessary, the regulations governing it are not obligatory. Therefore, one could imagine that one is simply omitting the ritual described in the Roman Missal, while one is inserting into the homily an activity that will bring home the homily's message of an ongoing attitude of mutual love and service among those who gather at the Lord's Supper.

The footwashing is described in the Missal as simply beginning, without any words of introduction or boundary remark to help people to move from the experience of listening to the gospel or the homily to that of movement and doing. So some formal words of introduction can help the smooth flow of the liturgy.[2]

Deacon, or some other person:

> Fellow servants of our Lord Jesus Christ,
> let us now proceed to carry out what he has taught us: that we, as his disciples, should wash one another's feet.

There is no need for words during the footwashing. People will normally talk to one another and this is a normal part of being a community. However, if some reflections are thought worthwhile, then the antiphons set out in the Roman Missal can be used, with individuals in various groups announcing them.

Given that Christ is present among us when we are engaged in footwashing, we should do nothing that could distract people from their activity—such as giving a running commentary. Similarly, creating a sense of rush or hurry is inappropriate. So music may help to create a calmer atmosphere. It is worth noting that the set of antiphons that make up the anthem *Ubi caritas et amor* was originally part of this Holy Thursday liturgy, and sums up the interrelated realities of mutual love and care, of being the people gathered in Christ, and of the presence of God among us.[3] However, variety is the spice of life and another even more ancient hymn is also a powerful hermeneutic of the action being performed if sung at this time. The so-called Philippians Hymn (Phil 2:6-11), with its stress on the mystery of the incarnation, celebrates God's relationship to our messy world. Moreover, it draws out the wonder that this earthy action of footwashing is not merely an ethical training in discipleship, but brings us into the mystery of the divine emptying.[4] *Kenosis* is one of those theological notions that seems both abstract and distant, and which rarely gets any liturgical exposure. The action, when interpreted through this hymn, may put us in touch with *kenosis* as both an insight into the divine mystery and a dimension of our discipleship.

The presider, the deacon, and any other ordained ministers should join one of the groups and both wash someone else's feet and have their own feet washed. It defeats the symbolism of mutual service if the ordained ministers behave any differently than other disciples.

When the washing is over, and when the basins, jugs, water, and towels have been cleared away, it is worth considering the inclusion of another element, directly linked with the new commandment of love: a collection for the poor. When princes and wealthy bishops performed this ceremony in the past they gave coins, and sometimes a meal, to a token number of poor men. But just as the footwashing should move from mime toward a greater reality as a human ritual, so care for the poor should move from being a token to a more actual involvement with the poor. Christian love is never inward-looking, but aims to reflect the bountiful divine love that is self-diffusive: if we really love one another, then that must spill over into care for the needy—and the most practical way that this can touch us while at liturgy is through a collection. It is worth recalling that we have evidence that a collection for the poor was an established practice at eucharistic meals by the mid-second century[5]—a collection for the poor administered by the presider rather than a collection in support of professional clergy—and it is an important element expressing the chain of divine love: God loves us, we love one another, we love the poor, the needy, the marginalized (1 John 4:20). So an announcement like this could be used:

The deacon:

> Long tradition has linked the new commandment to love and serve each other, the action of footwashing, with another practical expression of our love: care for the poor through sharing our wealth with them.
> So because care for the poor is one of the hallmarks of the people of God, there will now be a collection for the poor.

Then the presider receives the collection on behalf of the assembly.[6]

This part of the liturgy needs to be concluded with a prayer that acts as a focused conclusion to this part of the evening's liturgy. A prayer such as this:

The presider:

Father,
on this day your Son is teaching us that in acts of loving service toward one another we discover the mystery of your love.
Grant us, we pray, that through this footwashing we each may have a share in his life, and give us the strength we will need to carry on our lives as servants of one another,
for we ask this through Jesus Christ, our Lord.
Amen.

One other possibility is to vary the sequence of gospel > homily > footwashing to that of gospel > footwashing > homily. In the latter sequence the homily can act as an explication of and reflection upon the experience of the community.

Other Occasions for Footwashing

While having a true human event should be part of a celebration on Maundy Thursday, that which happens

only once a year—and on such a liturgically full day—
does not establish itself in our experience with the familiarity that allows us to appreciate it without being
so struck by its unusualness that we cannot get into its
implications. Here we have to be aware of a ritual tightrope: what rarely happens has greatest impact value;
but we can be so absorbed in the shock, we forget that
footwashing is but the starting point of a new way of
relating to one another. On the one hand, we have the
proverbial wisdom, noted by St. Augustine, that "What
we do every day, bores us" but on the other, we have
the historians' proverb, "That which happened once,
never happened!" We walk this tightrope in every area
of liturgy—the Eucharist being the outstanding example
—and so we need to have liturgical foothills to surround
the summit of Holy Thursday. Likewise, if the washing
is to go well on that day, some people in the gathering
need to be more generally familiar with it. Moreover,
since this is part of our Christian legacy, there are many
other occasions when a footwashing can be a powerful
liturgy, and one well authenticated from our traditions.

Commitment to Lent

Lent begins, midweek, with ashes. This is a wonderful ritual but one that many people miss out on because
it is midweek and going to church does not fit the week-
day schedule. Moreover, while ashes are a wonderful
sign of personal penitence, they do not bring out for us
either the need to begin to live in a new way—penitence

must be a new beginning and not just a payback for the past—or the community dimension of discipleship: we are called to live as a new *people* whose lives together are an anticipation of the kingdom. Furthermore, for those who were not there on Ash Wednesday, we need some event that marks the beginning of preparing for Easter that is more sensory than purple vestments and some words. A footwashing can be a balance to the message of Ash Wednesday, a marker of the beginning of Lent, and a real preparation for the celebration of the Holy Thursday liturgy.

Such a footwashing could take place after the homily on one of the Sundays of Lent, or, where RCIA is part of the community's ritual year, it can be presented as an experience of the kind of community—one of mutual service—that the candidates are preparing to enter. It could be introduced with:

Fellow servants in Christ Jesus,
on the evening before he entered into the paschal mystery
our Savior gave us an example of loving service and asked us to wash each other's feet.
As we prepare to celebrate the paschal mystery
[and welcome new members into our community of faith]
let us wash each other's feet, affirm our commitment to mutual service, and demonstrate what is involved in being members of the people of God.

As the people move around to get ready for the foot-washing, have someone read John 13:1-5 without any of the usual introductions.

If some words are needed during the washing, then individuals could proclaim the antiphons set out in the Roman Missal for Holy Thursday. But keep in mind that footwashing is an event in itself, a complete ritual action, and it does not need an overlay of words.

When people have finished washing feet, and the tidying up has taken place, read John 13:12-17. And then conclude:

> Let us pray,
> Father, as we set out on our Lenten journey we hear the call: be converted and believe in the good news. May this act of mutual respect and service help to renew us and give us a share in the life of Jesus Christ, your Son, our Lord. Amen.

Acts of Commissioning within the Community

A healthy community is one where the talents of each are mobilized and given creative space for the good of others: this is the interface between ecclesial need and individual vocation. But this is also the point at which notions of rank, and the equating of commissioning with power (as when we speak of commissions in an army), enter the church. That this is an endemic problem can be seen in the story in Mark 9:33-35:

Then they came to Capernaum; and when he was in the
house he asked [his disciples], "What were you arguing
about on the way?" But they were silent, for on the way they
had argued with one another about who was the greatest.
He sat down, called the twelve, and said to them, "Whoever wants to be first must be last of all and servant of all."

But the Jesus-based vision of a society is the very opposite of this notion of service as rank. This is the same
point that is being made in John 13 in the footwashing
by Jesus, and it is that which is being tested in 1 Timothy
5:10. It is not simply that the commissioned person is to
see oneself as a servant of the group (as distinct from
master of the group because of their particular skill),
but that everyone is to see oneself involved in mutual
service—and as such servants, they are equal.

So whether one is welcoming new people from outside a community—such as a new parish priest—or
asking individuals in the community to take on specific
tasks, be that eucharistic minister or member of the
finance committee, then a footwashing would be a
collective way of welcoming and recognizing the new
ministers, as well as creating an overall vision of the
ministry of the priestly people of God in which all
particular skills are given effect.

It might seem that here is a situation in which the
practice of one person washing the feet of many would
be appropriate. For example, a new parish priest would,
thereby, demonstrate, as should be the case, that he is
the *servus servorum Dei*. However, upon reflection we

should recognize that every individual ministry is for the good of all and must be part of the network of loving service. There are no absolute givers or takers in the community of the baptized, but all are sharers in the work of Christ. Similarly, it is easy for a gathering to feel that they are onlookers in any commissioning—as if they are outsourcing their responsibilities to a specialist—but a rite like footwashing does not allow such passivity: all must be active in service, some actions are done by all to each, and some, for example, presiding at the Eucharist, are only performed by an individual. Footwashing in such situations complements the specific ritual that relates to a group (e.g., appointing several new readers) or an individual (e.g., ordaining a deacon). The ritual could be introduced:

> The Lord Jesus gave us the paradigm of all ministry in the church when he washed his disciples' feet and told us that we ought to wash one another's feet. So as we welcome this/these new minister/s, let us reaffirm our understanding of what it is to belong to the community of love.

The text of John could then be used in two parts, along with the text from Mark; and the washing concluded:

> Father,
> may we embrace your Son's vision of loving service
> to one another and advance along the Way of Life.
> We ask this through Christ our Lord. Amen.

Renewal of Discipleship

One of the abiding insights of Catholic Christianity is that discipleship, faith in the Lord Jesus, is an ongoing affair, a pilgrimage not an arrival, a way not a destination, and one that involves continual renewal. This insight makes much of forgiveness stories in the gospels, such as Luke 15:4-7 or 19:1-10 or John 8:2-11, and the notion of the just person falling seven times and starting afresh (Prov 24:16). This corresponds to a human insight that we need to periodically start over, turn a page, or press the restart button. One liturgical expression that this takes is a renewal of baptismal promises, not just in the great moment of the Easter Vigil or on Easter Sunday, but on other occasions. But while we profess our faith in the church and the communion of saints, it remains an individual verbal affirmation, rather than collective affirmation of a community living the new life Jesus proclaimed as part of the people of covenant. Faith is not merely a public assent, but is living in community sharing in the life of the Lord.

This collective and participative aspect of discipleship needs to be given expression if it is to take root in us against the fissiparous individualism that reduces faith to a personal salvation cult. Some see such individualism as a particular tendency of the contemporary world or of consumerist culture, but, in reality, the temptation that faith be viewed in individualist terms is a deep-seated human proclivity. And one of the core themes of Christian liturgy is to challenge this view:

thus our basic actions when we thank the Father are to share a single loaf and drink from a common cup—alas we have individualized this long ago in such notions as "making my Communion" or "having a Mass said for my intentions"—and this is a theme that we find in foot-washing. Indeed, John in his gospel draws attention to it when he presents the need for Peter to engage with Jesus in footwashing as part of his having a share in him (13:8) and the final statement: "If you know" (note the plural: *oidate*) "these things, you are blessed" (note the plural: *makarioi este*) "if you do" (note the plural: *poiete*) "them" (13:17).

So a footwashing is an ideal complement to any liturgical act of renewing discipleship—though it would be inappropriate to hold it at either the Easter Vigil or on Easter Day as the footwashing on Maundy Thursday is part of the same liturgical moment. When the three questions professing faith have been answered, then the footwashing could be introduced with a statement such as:

> We have professed our faith in the communion of saints,
> now, following the example of Jesus who, though Lord and Teacher, got down and washed his disciples' feet,
> let us commit ourselves to the service and love of one another that follows from being sisters and brothers in the new covenant and wash each other's feet.

Other Community Events

A community that has discovered the value of foot-washing will discover that there are other moments in their life together when this action is an appropriate one to give bodily expression to their concerns. I have seen it used at meetings where it was part of catechetical days, at liturgy training workshops, at community building events, and particularly when a community has needed a ritual that could help heal wounds of division. Its very difficulty and its ability to bring people down to earth, literally, is part of its ritual power.

In such situations it is best not to celebrate it as part of a Eucharist—too many signals, too much ritual complexity, information overload—but just within the simplest of liturgical frames. When the people are sitting in groups ready to wash feet, a leader uses one of the standard openings (either "In the name of the Father and of the Son . . ." or "O God, come to our aid . . ."); then John 13:1-17 is read; then the washing takes place; that is followed by the Lord's Prayer; then a concluding prayer addressed to the Father, and one of the standard dismissals.

It can also be located within a Liturgy of the Word where the readings highlight the theme of the gathering, and John 13 read, perhaps in two sections during the actual washing to provide an anamnetic context to the deed. In communities that are familiar with the Liturgy of the Hours, a footwashing can easily be inserted into Evening Prayer after the psalmody and before the

Magnificat with the passage from John 13 used as the lection. It works particularly well within the even simpler office of Midday Prayer, where again it is inserted after the psalmody, John 13 being used as the lection, and the concluding prayer taken from the Liturgy of the Hours. However, take note of two points. First, if a community is not already familiar with the structure of the Liturgy of the Hours, then it is best to have the footwashing as a simple stand-alone ritual. Otherwise, there is too much unfamiliarity about what is happening next and concerns about finding places in books, and who should be saying what and when if the psalms are recited antiphonally. Second, do *not* use 1 Timothy 5:10 (with or without a verse either side to swell it out) in such a liturgy. It presupposes that the women in the assembly are willing to act as the servants, and no one else is mentioned! It therefore does not bring home a message of mutual service and could be interpreted to mean—as it most probably reflects—that some of the women in the church are expected to serve the men in the gathering. This is not an evangelical value, though perhaps it is only in our own time that we Christians see this clearly.

Penitential Liturgies

One of the major challenges facing the Catholic Church today, and in other ways all the churches, is to find a ritual of reconciliation and penitence. While this is not the place to examine the central issue, there are two aspects of liturgies of reconciliation that overlap with that of footwashing.

Most reconciliation rituals in the Western church since the disappearance of pastorally destructive public penance have so emphasized the individual, private aspects of penance and the notion of sin as an affront to God, that the social dimension of sin, the role of the community in reconciliation, and the need for reconciliation with each other in the community have all but disappeared. For centuries the image of penitence was that of escaping punishment, obtaining pardon, or becoming justified before God. Reconciliation with others, the need to rebuild community, the need to begin a new way of life with others became lost in the practicalities of restorative justice (i.e., repayment of material damage) and the footnotes to the theological justifications offered for the practice of indulgences. But a moment's reflection shows us that sin not only affects our relationship with God, but destroys the order within creation—and sin is far more complex, especially in its social dynamics, than most images of blotting one's record before a score-keeping God. Equally, if God's forgiveness is always available to those who seek it, the more pressing task is to seek the forgiveness of those who have been hurt by our actions. Seeking (and giving) forgiveness from one another is as much a consequence of hearing the gospel call to repent and believe as seeking divine forgiveness—and much more difficult. One way of bringing this social dimension of our sinfulness and of the ecclesial reconciliation is to see footwashing—which has a penitential undertone, as we see in the interchange between Jesus and Peter in John 13—as part of a penitential liturgy. Only in a new commitment to mutual service can we build a community where mercy and reconciliation are embedded.

The second problem relating to liturgies of reconciliation is that discussion tends to concentrate on two interconnected questions: individual confession versus general absolution. While this question has generated a complex canonical web ever since the publication of the reformed *Ordo Penitentiae* in 1973, the other problems with that ritual have often been ignored. Indeed, in many places of the Catholic Church reconciliation as a liturgy—distinct from an individual going to confession—has made almost no impression. One part of this problem is that there is no clear, public *action* connected with reconciliation as a *collective* event. Gathering, hearing readings, some prayers and then individual confession just seem like trimmings on the core activity of going to the confessional. This problem has attracted numerous solutions, such as asking people to write out their sins on paper and then burning the slips, but the ritual and theological problem remains. Each person needs to rebuild a set of relationships that we have damaged by our lack of love as much as we need divine grace to overcome our sinfulness. We all need to express the new way of living in community, and also to move away from a selfish theology where divine forgiveness is another commodity we need for ourselves!

These theological and ritual questions cannot be separated, nor can the search for the solution be divided between the canonists and the liturgists. One possible way forward is to place footwashing at the center of penitential services whereby in the new giving and taking, all become aware of the conflict between our "normal" world—snafu—and the world we seek as disciples of the Way. When linked with a liturgy of penance, it is not simply the case that footwashing is a powerful symbolic act, which it is, that makes it an appropriate action, but its more fundamental relationship to the place of reconciliation in the kerygma. Sinfulness is rooted in our societies in that we set high values on stratification and division, individual advancement at others' expense, and built into these postures is often the notion of exclusion that can take any number of forms. Any proclamation of reconciliation that does not confront these existing divisions is merely a contemporary expression of individualized salvation as preached by the Gnostics; so true liturgy, as the public work of the people of God, must challenge us to face all the kinds of division and exclusion with which we collude.

The fact is that we live in dysfunctional societies—and church communities—that are riven by distinctions based on wealth, ecclesiastical status, color, ethnicity, gender, and sexual orientation. Mutual footwashing challenges these divisions, calling on us to recognize our human commonality and equality as creatures, and the bonds that unite us, in Christ, as sisters and brothers in the Father's family. Accepting this challenge is the real issue, the *res tantum*, of the liturgical action. It is at the heart of any celebration of penance, of forgiveness, and of the starting again that flows from *metanoia*.

Ecumenical Liturgies

Liturgical celebrations that are specifically intended to bring together various traditions of Christianity in an act of common worship are, too often, overly verbal occasions: much text, many words, with some singing to form a "hymn sandwich." Such liturgies often betray their origins in a study: either the studies of the ministers involved or the studies of the sixteenth-century Reformers. They do not touch us in the way that community action involving us as bodily beings can touch us. Deep human rituals emerge from what communities do together. In an ideal world the celebration of our unity in faith would be for us all to eat together and bless the Father through, with, and in Jesus in the unity of the Holy Spirit as we share the loaf and cup. Alas, such a suggestion runs into canonical trouble among both Catholics and Orthodox. Moreover, differing views on who is validly ordained, or who could be ordained, or the nature of leadership in the churches can sometimes make anything other than words seem too problematic. And, there are many other Christians who feel they would be betraying their heritage if they imagined they were taking part in what Catholics would call a sacrament.

But a footwashing has many advantages in such situations. First, no one can claim it lacks biblical support. In the older language of controversy, it has "the surest warrants" of Scripture as a practice for the community. Second, it has a presence, albeit a peripheral presence generally, within all our traditions. Third, it has not been the subject of contention or theological controversy—so there is little bitter inheritance to be negotiated—and it has not been discussed in language that today still can generate more heat than light. Fourth, it is a practical ritual but one to which few "anti-ritualist" Christians can object, seeing as it is explicitly mandated in the *ipsissima verba* to which many such Christians are so deeply attached.[7] Fifth, it does not raise those issues that can undermine the logic of any genuine dialogical encounter, such as "who is really a member of the church?" or "who is really a member of the real church?" And, lastly, because of its traditional peripherality, it does not involve complex questions over who is empowered to do what or raise questions about ordination or leadership. By contrast, it does put forward a very definite image of what the whole community of Christians should be striving to become, and is a pointer to where each of them fall short. We have already noted the powerful effect that was produced when Jean Vanier introduced a footwashing and an Orthodox bishop knelt down and washed the feet of a woman Baptist minister.[8] Can you imagine any other ritual action, sanctioned by tradition among Christians, that would have facilitated this degree of shared action in Christ? This holds out to us a vision of what can be and that one day may be— and perhaps the place to start all ecumenical endeavors is on the floor of the church.

Here is a possible framework:

Introduction:

Christians share this memory of Jesus washing the feet of his disciples, showing them how they should relate to one another as his followers. Let us now, with Jesus present among us, wash each other's feet and discover afresh that we each have a share in him.

Read John 13:1-11 as people prepare for the footwashing; then when it is finished, John 13:12-16.

Conclusion:

Almighty, ever-living God, as we have washed each other's feet may we begin to learn the nature of the relationship of mutual love and service that should exist between us and all the disciples of your Son. May this action of washing each other's feet be a prayer in unity with his prayer to you: "that they may all be one; even as thou, Father, art in me, and

I in thee, that they also may be one in us, so that the
world may believe that thou hast sent me."
Amen.

It should always be kept in mind that when groups
do things together a real sense of unity is generated. I
suspect this is a consequence of our bodied nature: in-
teracting physically develops a visceral appreciation of
what is common to us, and a far greater feeling of our
unity than can be produced by any amount of reflection
or discussion. This is why singing together is better for
fostering a community than simply listening, and why
there is a greater sense of belonging among those who
play a team sport than within a discussion group. If we
can act in prayer together, then a very basic kind of
visible unity has already occurred.

Lastly, bear in mind that in some places people living
in interchurch families welcome the gesture of washing
each other's feet as compensation from feelings of exclusion due to not being allowed to share in the loaf and
cup.

Occasional Sunday Liturgies

When we read a gospel in the liturgy such as Mark
9:35-37—read on the Twenty-Fifth Sunday in Ordinary
Time of Year B[9]—on the nature of the relationships that
should exist among disciples, then the act of footwashing will link the memory being celebrated with the

demands of service far more effectively than a homilist's words. This theme, that the greatest in the community is to be the servant of all—in other words, that Jesus' community is to be one of radical equality—is also found in Mark 10:43-44, which is found in the gospel for the Twenty-Ninth Sunday in Ordinary Time of Year B, and so that Sunday is another occasion on which a footwashing is appropriate.[10] A community that has washed each other's feet often will generate a very different self-image of its relationship to the Good News than one that imagines itself merely sitting there listening to words.

Over the fifty years of the reformed Catholic liturgy many communities have recognized that sometimes an event within the Sunday liturgy, such as baptism, can bring new understanding to all who take part. One such event is a celebration of "the scandal of service."

Discovering an Action's Value

We may no longer need a basin, water, and a towel for our feet when we arrive in from the road, but practical expressions of caring and attention to one another still speak more eloquently than words. Actions of care, within our immediate communities, not only help establish a network of relationship among us, but show us that there can be another way, a way of peace and life, that is at the heart of discipleship. Christian liturgy exists to help bring that vision into reality as we welcome one another on the way, seek reconciliation with one another, and gather to share with one another in thanksgiving to the Father. But many of these bonds of community have become so stressed over the centuries that they fail to bring their message into focus, while becoming routines rather than moments allowing us to discover in Jesus' message new visions of life and community. Footwashing, because it is marginal in our tradition yet firmly located in the core of the gospel message, is a community event that holds out to us moments of discovery. Its history is theologically open, and so too is its future for those who explore its possibilities.

Notes

Chapter 1: Awkward Moments

1. See Peter Jeffery, "*Mandatum Novum Do Vobis*: Toward a Renewal of the Holy Thursday Footwashing Rite," *Worship* 64, no. 2 (1990): 107–41, for the background to this rubrical worry.

2. See Patricia Rumsey, "Women Have Feet, Too . . .," *The Pastoral Review* 9, no. 5 (2013): 51–54.

3. Allen Edgington, "Footwashing as an Ordinance," *Grace Theological Journal* 6 (1985): 425–34, is a good example of this approach, arguing that it is "an ordinance . . . to be perpetuated."

4. Janet M. Lindman, *Bodies of Belief: Baptist Community in Early America* (Philadelphia: University of Pennsylvania Press, 2008), 84–86.

5. Augustine, *Epistola* 55,18,33.

6. Adrian Howells, "Foot Washing for the Sole," *Performance Research: A Journal of the Performing Arts* 17 (2012): 128–31.

7. There were many variations in local practice, for it never rose to the "top level" of ritual. Adrian Fortescue, *The Ceremonies of the Roman Rite Described* (London: Burns, Oates and Washbourne, 1930), 313–15, mentions the washing of the right foot of thirteen poor men and then giving each a coin, but then adds: "This ceremony is generally now performed in cathedrals and religious houses only."

8. For more information: www.royalmint.com/discover/uk -coins/maundy-money (accessed April 12, 2015).

9. See Timothy Fry, ed., *Rule of Saint Benedict 1980* (Collegeville, MN: Liturgical Press, 1981), 35.1-14; 53.1-15; however, the translation used here is my own.

10. This verse is based on the Septuagint form of the psalms; the verse is now rendered, "We ponder your steadfast love, O God, / in the midst of your temple" (Ps 48:9).

11. See Susan E. Von Daum Tholl, "Life according to the Rule: A Monastic Modification of *Mandatum* Imagery in the Peterborough Psalter," *Gesta* 33 (1994): 151–58.

12. See G.S.M. Walker, *Sancti Columbani Opera* (Dublin: Dublin Institute for Advanced Studies, 1957), 180–81.

13. Mennonite Church of Canada, "Confession of Faith," article 13, http://home.mennonitechurch.ca/cof/art.13.

14. John D. Rempel, "The Lord's Supper in Mennonite Tradition," *Vision: A Journal for Church and Theology* 2 (2001): 8–10 and 13.

15. Keith Graber-Miller, "Mennonite Footwashing: Identity Reflections and Altered Meanings," *Worship* 66 (1992): 148–70 is an excellent summary of how footwashing has formed Mennonite identity.

16. Bob Brenneman, "Embodied Forgiveness: Yoder and the (Body) Politics of Footwashing," *Mennonite Quarterly Review* 83 (2009): 7–28.

17. John D. Roth, *Practices: Mennonite Worship and Witness* (Scottdale, PA: Herald Press, 2009), 103–23.

18. Thomas O'Loughlin, *The Didache: A Window on the Earliest Christians* (Grand Rapids, MI: Baker Academic, 2010), 105–28.

19. Jean Vanier, *The Scandal of Service: Jesus Washes Our Feet* (Toronto: Novalis, 1996), 86.

20. Quotations are from Catherine Anderson and Sandra Carroll, "The Foot-Washing in John 13:1-20 in the Context of *L'Arche*," *Australian eJournal of Theology* 20, no. 3 (2013): 185–96.

21. Thomas O'Loughlin, "Translating *Panis* in a Eucharistic Context: A Problem of Language and Theology," *Worship* 78 (2004): 226–35.

22. WCC press release printed in *Letters of L'Arche* 97 (1998): 7.

23. Jean Vanier, *Drawn into the Mystery of Jesus through the Gospel of John* (Ottawa: Novalis, 2004), 230.

24. Sen Sendjaya and James C. Sarros, "Servant Leadership: Its Origin, Development, and Application in Organizations," *Journal of Leadership and Organizational Studies* 9, no. 2 (2002): 57–64.

25. Madge Karecki, "Clare of Assisi: Foot-Washing Leadership," Regent University, www.regent.edu/acad/global/publications /innerresources/vol1iss1/Karecki_Clare.pdf (accessed April 1, 2015).

Chapter 2: An Action by Jesus?

1. Gen 19:2; 24:32; 43:24; and Judg 19:21.

2. G.A. Frank Knight, "Feet-washing," in *Encyclopaedia of Religion and Ethics*, ed. James Hastings, vol. 5, 814–23 (Edinburgh: T. and T. Clark, 1912)—still the best survey listing historical evidence for the practice; and see Harold Weiss, "Footwashing," in *The Anchor Bible Dictionary*, ed. David N. Freedman, vol. 2, 828–29 (New York: Doubleday, 1992), for a summary.

3. Plato, *The Symposium* 175.

4. To see a beautiful example, look up "footbath" on the website of New York's Metropolitan Museum of Art. For the background to this footbath see Marjorie J. Milne, "A Greek Footbath in the Metropolitan Museum of Art," *American Journal of Archaeology* 48 (1944): 26–63.

5. The footwashing is mentioned in Text A 6,6 and Text B 3,9 (and on Abraham's hospitality in general see A 1,5 and 4,6 and B 2,10). The texts can be found in E.P. Sanders, "The Testament of Abraham," in *The Old Testament Pseudepigrapha*, ed. James H. Charlesworth, vol. 1, 871–902 (London: Darton, Longman and Todd, 1983).

6. 13,15 and 20,1-5. The text can be found in C. Burchard, "Joseph and Aseneth," in *The Old Testament Pseudepigrapha*, ed. James H. Charlesworth, vol. 2, 177–247 (London: Darton, Longman and Todd, 1985).

7. Thomas O'Loughlin, *The Eucharist: Origins and Contemporary Understandings* (London: Bloomsbury, 2015), 166–76.

8. See Étienne Nodet and Justin Taylor, *The Origins of Christianity: An Exploration* (Collegeville, MN: Liturgical Press, 1998) for an

elaboration of this method; and Thomas O'Loughlin, "Liturgical Evolution and the Fallacy of the Continuing Consequence," *Worship* 83 (2009): 312–23.

9. Stanislao Loffreda, *Holy Land Pottery at the Time of Jesus: Early Roman Period 63 BC–70 AD* (Jerusalem: Franciscan Printing Press, 2002), 10–11.

10. See Ingrid R. Kitzberger, "Love and Footwashing: John 13:1-20 and Luke 7:36-50 Read Intertextually," *Biblical Interpretation* 2, no. 2 (1994): 190–205; and Thomas O'Loughlin, "Harmonizing the Anointings of the Christ: Eusebius and the Four-Gospel Problem," *Milltown Studies* 73 (2014): 1–17.

11. Richard Bauckham, *The Testimony of the Beloved Disciple: Narrative, History, and Theology in the Gospel of John* (Grand Rapids, MI: Baker Academic, 2007), 203.

12. See James D. G. Dunn, "The Washing of the Disciples' Feet in John 13:1-20," *Zeitschrift für die Neutestamentliche Wissenschaft* 61 (1970): 247–52.

13. For example, Raymond E. Brown, *The Gospel According to John* (New York: Doubleday, 1966), 558–72; Rudolf Bultmann, *The Gospel of John* (Oxford: Blackwell, 1971), 463–79; and Francis J. Moloney, *The Gospel of John* (Collegeville, MN: Liturgical Press, 1998), 372–79.

14. See Jean Vanier, *Drawn into the Mystery of Jesus through the Gospel of John* (Ottawa: Novalis, 2004), 223–39.

15. Bauckham, *The Testimony of the Beloved Disciple*, 195.

16. See Eric W. Rothenbuhler, *Ritual Communication: From Everyday Conversation to Mediated Ceremony* (Thousand Oaks, CA: Sage, 1998).

17. See, for example, John C. Thomas, *Footwashing in John 13 and the Johannine Community* (Sheffield: Sheffield Academic Press, 1991); and Frank D. Macchia, "Is Footwashing the Neglected Sacrament? A Theological Response to John Christopher Thomas," *Pneuma* 19 (1997): 239–49.

18. This will be explored, in chap. 5, as part of the value of footwashing in ecumenical celebrations.

19. See Edward Schillebeeckx, *Christ the Sacrament of the Encounter with God* (London: Sheed and Ward, 1963).

20. See Joseph Martos, *Doors to the Sacred: A Historical Introduction to Sacraments in the Catholic Church* (Liguori, MO: Liguori Publications, 2014).

Chapter 3: Mystagogy, Memory, and Meaning

1. Keith Graber-Miller, "Mennonite Footwashing: Identity Reflections and Altered Meanings," *Worship* 66 (1992): 148–70.

2. See Thomas O'Loughlin, "The Liturgical Vessels of the Latin Eucharistic Liturgy: A Case of an Embedded Theology," *Worship* 82 (2008): 482–504.

3. For an introduction to this topic, see Barry Schwartz, "The Social Context of Commemoration: A Study in Collective Memory," *Social Forces* 61 (1982): 374–402; or Paul Connerton, *How Societies Remember* (Cambridge: Cambridge University Press, 1989).

4. A very good example of this approach can be found in Sandra M. Schneiders, "The Foot Washing (John 13:1-20): An Experiment in Hermeneutics," *Catholic Biblical Quarterly* 43 (1981): 76–92.

5. Cf. Theodore W. Jennings, "On Ritual Knowledge," *Journal of Religion* 62, no. 2 (1982): 111–27.

6. It is worth looking at the devastating critique of actual liturgical practice by Adrian Howells, "Foot Washing for the Sole," *Performance Research: A Journal of the Performing Arts* 17 (2012): 128–31, who views it from the standpoint of a performance artist.

7. We have been making this mistake since then because of the veil of Latin. Once the liturgy had to be mediated to most Christians through explanations *other than actual participations* there arose the distinct levels of (1) what was being done, (2) what was claimed in the explanations for what was being done, and (3) the significance assigned by people to their own experience.

8. For an account of these ceremonies one has to go back to nineteenth-century descriptions such as Cardinal Nicholas Wiseman, *Four Lectures on the Offices and Services of Holy Week as Performed in the Papal Chapels* (Baltimore: J. Murphy & Co., 1854), 72–73; or Henry J. Feasey, *Ancient English Holy Week Ceremonial* (London: Thomas Baker, 1897), 107–12.

9. This point was made by Martin Luther in his criticism of the practice of footwashing; see Graber-Miller, "Mennonite Footwashing," 158, n. 34.

10. See Schneiders, "The Foot Washing (John 13:1-20)."

11. For a full study of this point, see Thomas O'Loughlin, "The Washing of Feet: The Interplay of Praxis and Theology," *Anaphora* 7, no. 1 (2013): 37–46.

12. The Latin text can be most conveniently found in G.A. Frank Knight, "Feet-washing," in *Encyclopaedia of Religion and Ethics*, ed. James Hastings, vol. 5, 816 (Edinburgh: T. and T. Clark, 1912).

Chapter 4: Getting Down to It

1. It is best to go to the right, as most people are right-handed and this facilitates moving jugs and basins on the floor.

2. Fetching water is also an expression of mutual service in the community: cf. Josh 9:21-27.

3. See Adrian Howells, "Foot Washing for the Sole," *Performance Research: A Journal of the Performing Arts* 17 (2012): 128–31.

4. On this conflation of various footwashings and anointings, see Thomas O'Loughlin, "Harmonizing the Anointings of the Christ: Eusebius and the Four-Gospel Problem," *Milltown Studies* 73 (2014): 1–17.

5. Bishops' Committee on the Liturgy, *Music in Catholic Worship* (Washington, DC: National Conference of Catholic Bishops, 1972), 6. See also the evolution of this passage in three other documents— *The Place of Music in Eucharistic Celebration* (1968); *Music in Catholic Worship*, rev. ed. (1983); and *Sing to the Lord* (2007)—as described in Edward Foley, *A Lyrical Vision: The Music Documents of the US Bishops*, American Essays in Liturgy (Collegeville, MN: Liturgical Press, 2009), 22, 32–33, 43, 61.

Chapter 5: Liturgical Scenarios

1. See the valuable discussion in John M. Huels, *More Disputed Questions in Liturgy* (Chicago: Liturgy Training Publications, 1996),

25–27, where he shows, working from the principles of canonical interpretation, that *viri* should be understood in terms of the liturgy's core values and "the equality of all the baptised [which] is a principle enshrined in the fundamental, constitutional law of the church (canon 208). This principle is based on divine law, to which merely ecclesiastical (human) law must defer" (p. 27). Huels's overall positioning of liturgical law and rubrics within a larger framework of eleven core principles of liturgical action (pp. 13–21) is a valuable antidote to rubrical fundamentalism.

2. I want to acknowledge getting some ideas for what is given here from the Church of England's *Common Worship*, Times and Seasons volume, 298; and the Episcopal Church of the USA's *Book of Occasional Services 2003*, 93.

3. In the Tridentine Missal, this set of antiphons was given as part of the footwashing ceremony that took place either after the Eucharist was finished, indeed after the stripping of the altars, or in a ceremony entirely separate from the Eucharist. In the 1956 Order of Holy Week it was included as the final sung element of the footwashing, now located in the evening Eucharist, but in the 1969 Missal it kept the same textual location but was interpreted as a hymn that coincided with the procession for the poor and the beginning of the Liturgy of the Eucharist—and as such was easily displaced by an offertory hymn. It is a gem of the tradition that belongs to the footwashing; and if it is used, then the best place is during the footwashing. It is worth noting that the normal sung form of refrain is *Ubi caritas et amor*—that God is present in both *agape* and *eros*—and this is the form found in the liturgical books until 1969. The current Latin text has *ubi caritas est vera* (where there is genuine *caritas*), manifesting a rather hesitant view of the incarnation, or that God's presence suffuses the creation *and* our human experience.

4. I am indebted to Bernadette Gasslein for drawing my attention to this point.

5. This is what Justin writes: "Then [when they have finished sharing the loaf and cup] those who are wealthy, and willing, give whatever each thinks fit, and what is collected is left with the presider who uses it to help widows and orphans and anyone else who is in

need be that due to sickness or some other problem, and also those among us who are slaves or strangers staying with us; in short, he cares for all those who are in need" (*First Apology* 67,6–7).

6. In the Roman Missal this collection is mentioned indirectly in the first rubric relating to the Liturgy of the Eucharist that "there may possibly be a procession of the faithful with gifts for the poor." However, if this collection—different in destination from that of most collections at the liturgy—is brought within the footwashing part of the liturgy, the links of love/charity/*agape* are better expressed.

7. I place quotation marks around "anti-ritualist" as I firmly believe that ritual is at the heart of all human communication, be it a handshake or the conventions around a shared cup of coffee. To be human is to engage in ritual!

8. Catherine Anderson and Sandra Carroll, "The Foot-Washing in John 13:1-20 in the Context of *L'Arche*," *Australian eJournal of Theology* 20, no. 3 (2013): 196.

9. The parallels to this passage of Mark's gospel (i.e., Matt 18:1-5 and Luke 9:46-48) are not set out in the Lectionary for Ordinary Time.

10. The parallels to this passage (i.e., Matt 20:24-28 and Luke 22:24-27) are not set out in the Lectionary for Ordinary Time.

Bibliography

Anderson, Catherine, and Sandra Carroll. "The Foot-Washing in John 13:1-20 in the Context of *L'Arche.*" *Australian eJournal of Theology* 20, no. 3 (2013): 185–96.

Bauckham, Richard. *The Testimony of the Beloved Disciple: Narrative, History, and Theology in the Gospel of John.* Grand Rapids, MI: Baker Academic, 2007.

Brenneman, Bob. "Embodied Forgiveness: Yoder and the (Body) Politics of Footwashing." *Mennonite Quarterly Review* 83 (2009): 7–28.

Brown, Raymond E. *The Gospel According to John.* New York: Doubleday, 1966.

Bultmann, Rudolf. *The Gospel of John.* Translated by G.R. Beasley-Murray. Oxford: Blackwell, 1971.

Burchard, C. "Joseph and Aseneth." In *The Old Testament Pseudepigrapha*, edited by James H. Charlesworth, vol. 2, 177–247. London: Darton, Longman and Todd, 1985.

Connerton, Paul. *How Societies Remember.* Cambridge: Cambridge University Press, 1989.

Dunn, James D. G. "The Washing of the Disciples' Feet in John 13:1-20." *Zeitschrift für die Neutestamentliche Wissenschaft* 61 (1970): 247–52.

Edgington, Allen. "Footwashing as an Ordinance," *Grace Theological Journal* 6 (1985): 425–34.

Feasey, Henry J. *Ancient English Holy Week Ceremonial*. London: Thomas Baker, 1897.

Fortescue, Adrian. *The Ceremonies of the Roman Rite Described*. 3rd ed., with assistance from J.B. O'Connell. London: Burns, Oates and Washbourne, 1930.

Graber-Miller, Keith. "Mennonite Footwashing: Identity Reflections and Altered Meanings." *Worship* 66 (1992): 148–70.

Howells, Adrian. "Foot Washing for the Sole." *Performance Research: A Journal of the Performing Arts* 17 (2012): 128–31.

Huels, John M. *More Disputed Questions in Liturgy*. Chicago: Liturgy Training Publications, 1996.

Jeffery, Peter. "*Mandatum Novum Do Vobis*: Toward a Renewal of the Holy Thursday Footwashing Rite," *Worship* 64, no. 2 (1990): 107–41.

Jennings, Theodore W. "On Ritual Knowledge." *Journal of Religion* 62, no. 2 (1982): 111–27.

Kitzberger, Ingrid R. "Love and Footwashing: John 13:1-20 and Luke 7:36-50 Read Intertextually." *Biblical Interpretation* 2, no. 2 (1994): 190–205.

Knight, G.A. Frank. "Feet-washing." In *Encyclopaedia of Religion and Ethics*, edited by James Hastings, vol. 5, 814–23. Edinburgh: T. and T. Clark, 1912.

Lindman, Janet M. *Bodies of Belief: Baptist Community in Early America*. Philadelphia: University of Pennsylvania Press, 2008.

Loffreda, Stanislao. *Holy Land Pottery at the Time of Jesus: Early Roman Period 63 BC–70 AD*. Jerusalem: Franciscan Printing Press, 2002.

Macchia, Frank D. "Is Footwashing the Neglected Sacrament? A Theological Response to John Christopher Thomas." *Pneuma* 19 (1997): 239–49.

Martos, Joseph. *Doors to the Sacred: A Historical Introduction to Sacraments in the Catholic Church*. Vatican II Golden Anniversary Edition. Liguori, MO: Liguori Publications, 2014.

Milne, Marjorie J. "A Greek Footbath in the Metropolitan Museum of Art." *American Journal of Archaeology* 48 (1944): 26–63.

Moloney, Francis J. *The Gospel of John*. Collegeville, MN: Liturgical Press, 1998.

Nodet, Étienne, and Justin Taylor. *The Origins of Christianity: An Exploration*. Collegeville, MN: Liturgical Press, 1998.

O'Loughlin, Thomas. *The Didache: A Window on the Earliest Christians*. Grand Rapids, MI: Baker Academic, 2010.

———. *The Eucharist: Origins and Contemporary Understandings*. London: Bloomsbury, 2015.

———. "From a Damp Floor to a New Vision of Church: Footwashing as a Challenge to Liturgy and Discipleship." *Worship* 88, no. 2 (2014): 137–50.

———. "Harmonizing the Anointings of the Christ: Eusebius and the Four-Gospel Problem." *Milltown Studies* 73 (2014): 1–17.

———. "Liturgical Evolution and the Fallacy of the Continuing Consequence." *Worship* 83 (2009): 312–23.

———. "The Liturgical Vessels of the Latin Eucharistic Liturgy: A Case of an Embedded Theology." *Worship* 82 (2008): 482–504.

———. "The Washing of Feet: The Interplay of Praxis and Theology." *Anaphora* 7, no. 1 (2013): 37–46.

Rempel, John D. "The Lord's Supper in Mennonite Tradition." *Vision: A Journal for Church and Theology* 2 (2001): 4–15.

Roth, John D. *Practices: Mennonite Worship and Witness*. Scottdale, PA: Herald Press, 2009.

Rothenbuhler, Eric W. *Ritual Communication: From Everyday Conversation to Mediated Ceremony*. Thousand Oaks, CA: Sage, 1998.

Rule of Saint Benedict 1980. Edited by Timothy Fry. Collegeville, MN: Liturgical Press, 1981.

Rumsey, Patricia. "Women Have Feet, Too . . ." *The Pastoral Review* 9, no. 5 (2013): 51–54.

Sanders, E.P. "The Testament of Abraham." In *The Old Testament Pseudepigrapha*, edited by James H. Charlesworth, vol. 1, 871–902. London: Darton, Longman and Todd, 1983.

Schillebeeckx, Edward. *Christ the Sacrament of the Encounter with God*. London: Sheed and Ward, 1963.

Schneiders, Sandra M. "The Foot Washing (John 13:1-20): An Experiment in Hermeneutics." *Catholic Biblical Quarterly* 43 (1981): 76–92.

Schwartz, Barry. "The Social Context of Commemoration: A Study in Collective Memory." *Social Forces* 61 (1982): 374–402.

Sendjaya, Sen, and James C. Sarros. "Servant Leadership: Its Origin, Development, and Application in Organizations." *Journal of Leadership and Organizational Studies* 9, no. 2 (2002): 57–64.

Thomas, John C. *Footwashing in John 13 and the Johannine Community*. Sheffield: Sheffield Academic Press, 1991.

Vanier, Jean. *Drawn into the Mystery of Jesus through the Gospel of John*. Ottawa: Novalis, 2004.

———. *The Scandal of Service: Jesus Washes Our Feet*. Toronto: Novalis, 1996.

Von Daum Tholl, Susan E. "Life according to the Rule: A Monastic Modification of *Mandatum* Imagery in the Peterborough Psalter." *Gesta* 33 (1994): 151–58.

Walker, G.S.M. *Sancti Columbani Opera*. Dublin: Dublin Institute for Advanced Studies, 1957.

Weiss, Harold. "Footwashing." In *The Anchor Bible Dictionary*, edited by David N. Freedman, vol. 2, 828–29. New York: Doubleday, 1992.

Wiseman, Nicholas. *Four Lectures on the Offices and Services of Holy Week as Performed in the Papal Chapels*. Baltimore: J. Murphy & Co., 1854.